Guyana

Guyana

BY MARION MORRISON

Enchantment of the World
Second Series

Children's Press®

A Division of Scholastic Inc.

NEW YORK   TORONTO   LONDON   AUCKLAND   SYDNEY
MEXICO CITY   NEW DELHI   HONG KONG
DANBURY, CONNECTICUT

Frontispiece: Canoeing on the Rupununi River

Consultant: Dr. Kalowatie Deonandan, Chair, International Studies Program, University of Saskatchewan, Saskatoon, Canada

Please note: *All statistics are as up-to-date as possible at the time of publication.*

Book production by Herman Adler Design

Library of Congress Cataloging-in-Publication Data

Morrison, Marion.
  Guyana / by Marion Morrison.
    p. cm. — (Enchantment of the world. Second series)
    Includes bibliographical references and index.
    ISBN 0-516-22377-1
    1. Guyana—juvenile literature. [1. Guyana.] I. Title. II. Series.
F2368.5 .M67 2004
988.1—dc21   2001006915

Acknowledgments

The author would like to thank the following people and organizations for their help in preparing this book: Dr. Jevan Berrangé, Dr. Conrad Gorinsky, the McTurk family, Karanambo, Jason Howe, the library of the Royal Geographical Society, and the library at Canning House, London.

Contents

Cover photo:
Kaieteur Falls

CHAPTER

Village life

A wood carving

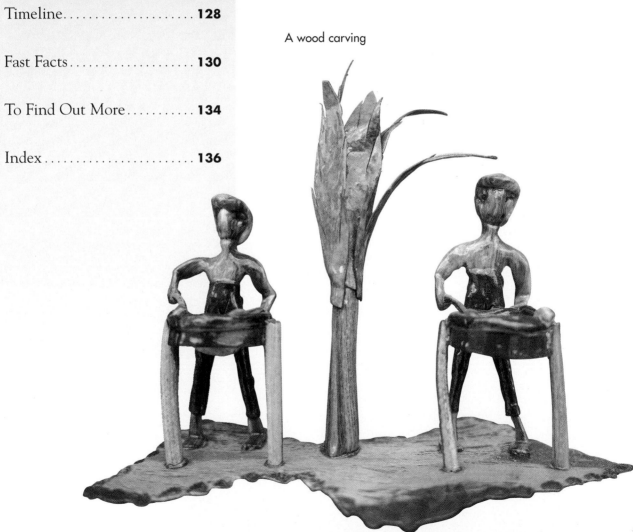

Lost Worlds

LONG BEFORE WHITE MEN SET FOOT IN THE NEW WORLD, its land was inhabited by tribes with their own legendary myths of creation. One of these tribes, the Arawak, believed that in the beginning *Aiomun Kondi*, the Dweller in the Height, made the earth. Although the waves beat upon the shore and the breezes sighed gently over the land, no life was to be seen. Then Aiomun Kondi caused the wonderful silk-cotton tree to grow, whose branches reached into the clouds. From this green throne he scattered twigs and bark, some into the air, some onto the land, and some on the sparkling waters. Those that fell upon the waters became shining fish darting hither and thither. Those that remained in the air became winged and feathered fowl, and those that fell on the ground turned into beasts and reptiles and men and women, spreading to fill the whole earth.

Opposite: **The uninhabited jungle of Guyana**

Ancient Amerindians fished the rivers of the interior.

When Europeans first arrived on the northeast coast of South America early in the sixteenth century, they found Arawaks and other Amerindian tribes. Over the centuries, the Amerindians had survived by hunting and fishing. But the Europeans found the region

uninviting, covered by thick coastal mangrove swamps and dense rain forests. They called it the "wild coast," and few of them settled there. The territory might have been ignored altogether had there not been legends and rumors of a "lost world" that promised gold and great fortunes. So the hunt began for the legendary *El Dorado*, or "Golden King," and Manoa, his golden city. It was said that every year the king dived into a lake, his body covered with gold. He would emerge naked, leaving the gold on the lake bed.

A Spaniard named Juan Martínez, who was captured by Amerindians and lived with them for ten years, was convinced he had seen the lake and the city in the region of the Rupununi Savanna in what is now Guyana. Expeditions soon followed. Spanish, German, and British explorers, including Sir Walter Raleigh, went in search of it, but no one found the lost world of Manoa.

Early explorers searched for the "lost world."

Switch now to the late nineteenth century and a distinguished assembly of explorers and scientists at the renowned Royal Geographical Society in London. There, Professor Challenger is giving a lecture to the astonished assembly about a lost world of prehistoric animals, ape-men, and exotic plants from which he and his colleagues had just escaped. At one point he lets one of these terrifying animals loose. It flies across the room, causing the assembly to rush for the doors.

Mount Roraima is thought to be the inspiration for the novel *The Lost World*.

This, of course, is all fiction. The story comes from *The Lost World*, a classic Victorian novel written by Sir Arthur Conan Doyle, best known as the creator of the detective Sherlock Holmes. What is of interest here, though, is that the world in which Challenger and his colleagues became lost is thought by many to be based on Mount Roraima, which is on the border of Guyana, Venezuela, and Brazil. Roraima is a truly awesome mountain that looms over the savanna, its flat-topped summit permanently hidden in swirling mist. The sides of the mountain are thick with tropical trees and plants, and curious shapes in the rock could easily be mistaken for strange creatures. It was discovered in 1838, a time when European and American explorers and scientists were visiting for the first time some of the most remote, unknown parts of the South American continent.

In some ways Guyana is still something of a lost world. Fewer than a million people live there. The majority live in Georgetown, the capital; in two or three other small towns; and along the coast. Amerindians and a tiny number of settlers, most of them miners or loggers, live in the interior.

Great areas of mountain, savanna, and rain forest in Guyana are virtually uninhabited. Until the airplane arrived, getting around the interior was almost entirely by river and involved long, dangerous journeys. The isolation of the interior has

Guyanese society is a blend of people from many parts of the world.

been a fortunate protection for the vast number of creatures living there. The forests are alive with all kinds of colorful, noisy birds; mammals ranging from monkeys and jaguars to less well-known tapirs, capybaras, and anteaters; and thousands of species of insects.

The people of Guyana have come from many parts of the world. Only the Amerindians are native to the region. The first Europeans to arrive in Guyana were Spanish, Dutch, French, and British, with the British obtaining possession of the country. During the eighteenth and nineteenth centuries, black African slaves, East Indians, Portuguese, and Chinese laborers were brought in to work the land. For a long time, the African population was the majority, but today there are more East Indians. Guyanese society is divided, especially in the field of politics.

The British created the colony of British Guiana in 1831. It became independent in 1966 and since then has been governed by one of two political parties. For the first twenty-six years it was the People's National Congress, largely supported by the Afro-Guyanese (Africans), and since 1992 it has been the People's Progressive Party, supported by the Indo-Guyanese (East Indians). The future of Guyana depends on these two parties bridging the gap between them to work for the common good.

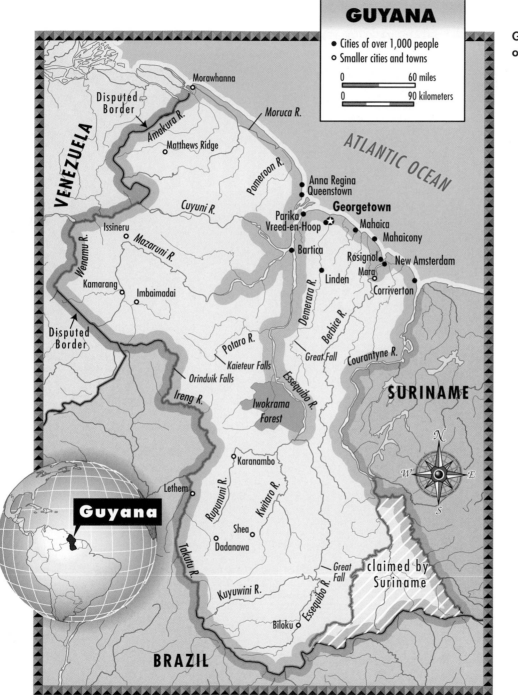

GUYANA

- ● Cities of over 1,000 people
- ○ Smaller cities and towns

0   60 miles

0   90 kilometers

Geopolitical map of Guyana

ATLANTIC OCEAN

VENEZUELA

Disputed Border

Morawhanna

Amakura R.

Moruca R.

Matthews Ridge

Pomeroon R.

Cuyuni R.

Anna Regina
Queenstown

Georgetown

Parika
Vreed-en-Hoop

Mahaica

Mahaicony

Issineru

Wenamu R.

Mazaruni R.

Bartica

Rosignol

New Amsterdam

Linden

Mara

Corriverton

Kamarang

Imbaimadai

Demerara R.

Berbice R.

Disputed Border

Potaro R.

Kaieteur Falls

Great Fall

Courantyne R.

Orinduik Falls

Essequibo R.

Ireng R.

SURINAME

Iwokrama
Forest

N

W   E

S

Karanambo

Rupununi R.

Kwitaro R.

Lethem

Guyana

Shea

Dadanawa

Great
Fall

claimed by
Suriname

Takutu R.

Kuyuwini R.

Essequibo R.

Biloku

BRAZIL

The Land of Waters

Guyana is one of three small countries, known collectively as the Guianas, on the northeastern seaboard of South America. The country's official name is the Cooperative Republic of Guyana. It is about the size of Idaho and is the fourth-smallest country in South America. To the west, the country is flanked almost equally by Venezuela and by Brazil, South America's largest country. Brazil also touches all of the southern border. Suriname, once Dutch Guiana, lies to the east.

A low-lying, often muddy Atlantic coast runs diagonally northwest to southeast. Tropical forests of different kinds cover much of the country, with variations of altitude and soil influencing the types of trees that grow. Much of the central southern area is open savanna grassland and in places is very flat. Flat-topped mountains, including Mount Roraima, rise across the western side, but elsewhere the land is relatively low. Mountain ranges such as the Acaraí rise as high as 2,000 feet (610 meters) in the south and form the divide between streams flowing south to the Amazon system and those flowing north into the heart of Guyana.

Few places are blessed with so many rivers, creeks, and swamps. The original people knew it as the "land of water." The longest river, the Essequibo, extends 630 miles (1,014 kilometers)

Opposite: **Most people still travel by canoe in the interior of Guyana.**

The Essequibo is the longest river in Guyana.

from the far south to the north, running through the country like the trunk of a tree with numerous tributaries on either side resembling branches. On each side of the Essequibo River, Guyana stretches no more than 190 miles (306 km), and sometimes far less, to its neighbors. Two major tributaries of the Essequibo, the Mazaruni and the Cuyuni, flow from sources in the west. They enter the main stream at the small town of Bartica approximately 40 miles (64 km) from the sea.

The Demerara River, which runs to the east of the Essequibo, is the country's most important river because it carries the giant ore ships from the bauxite mines of Linden. Georgetown, the capital, stands at its mouth on the east bank. The Courantyne River, which also flows to the Atlantic, forms the border with Suriname. Smaller rivers such as the Berbice in the east and the Barima in the northwest also flow to the Atlantic.

The Essequibo River is fed by other rivers from more than half of Guyana and sets the scene for the whole country. The middle course flows through flat, open savanna country lined with forests of tall palms. On the western horizon, the low Kanuku Mountains peek through the clouds. In the other direction, toward Suriname, water remaining from the rainy season covers the bed of an ancient lake that sometimes extends as far as the eye can see. Countless rock drawings, or petroglyphs, made centuries ago by Amerindians

Petroglyphs, or rock drawings, tell the history of nearby rivers.

by scratching on riverside boulders recall the history of the river. They used the river as a highway to the interior and to Amazonia regions along rivers flowing south from the Acaraí Mountains.

The coastline of the Guianas originally extended along present-day Guyana, Suriname (formerly Dutch Guiana), and French Guiana. Today, this area of Guyana is not very impressive. Many miles of sandy or muddy beaches are backed by shallow dunes often held in place by a spreading cover of plants. Behind the shore, palm trees have been planted. In some parts an artificial seawall has been built to protect the land. A narrow coastal plain, from about 2 to 30 miles (3.2 to 48 km) across at the widest point, which lies immediately

Fields for farming lie along the coast.

behind the shore, has been influenced considerably by farming activity. This coastal strip is of prime economic importance. Roads and agricultural buildings dominate extensive fields whose water is controlled by canals and sluice gates.

Where rivers such as the Essequibo enter the sea, only remnants of mangrove forests fringe the coast. Almost everywhere there are signs of settlement, especially near the capital, Georgetown, and southward to Linden, the country's second-largest city.

Looking at Guyana's Cities

Linden is best described as the bauxite capital, for it is from here that mineral is exported directly from the mines (below). It is a disconcerting experience to be in a small boat on the Demerara River and round a bend to come face to face with an oceangoing ore transporter. Linden was created in 1970 by bringing together the three smaller towns of Wismar, Christianborg, and Mackenzie. The town of Mackenzie was founded originally by George Bain Mackenzie, an American geologist of Scottish descent. Mackenzie arrived in Guyana in 1913 to search for valuable minerals. He established a bauxite mine for the Public Mining and Manufacturing Company of Philadelphia. Mackenzie became ill in the tropical climate and returned to the United States in 1915, to die soon after. Linden is now second in importance to Georgetown.

New Amsterdam, on the eastern bank of the Berbice River, has a population of little more than 25,000. Leafy streets lend an unhurried atmosphere to this old Dutch settlement. A good road connects New Amsterdam to Georgetown and to Corriverton, a border town on the Courantyne River 30 miles (48 km) to the southwest.

At another extreme is Lethem, a small town on the eastern bank of the Takutu River bordering Brazil. The town has a small airport; connections to the interior of Guyana are by dusty roads. An easy walk in the opposite direction leads to a river ferry, which crosses to Bonfim in Brazil.

The Real Guyana

It is often said that the "real Guyana" begins inland, away from the coast. The thought of lost worlds is never far off, and while prehistoric animals may not live there today, this part of South America has some of the oldest rock formations on the continent. Millions of years ago the land was part of one of the earth's two supercontinents. Slowly they drifted apart, until the continents as we know them today were formed.

As South America changed, mountains such as the Andes grew, while sediment from erosion or the sea spread across much of the eastern side of the continent. In Guyana and neighboring countries, some of the rocks of the ancient super-continent have remained on the surface, standing as eye-catching mountains. This region is known geologically as the Brazilian and Guiana Highlands, and its crystalline rocks are a reminder of a fiery origin.

White Sands

Once away from the coast, it is easy to see how the land has been influenced by ancient geological features. About 40 miles (64 km) from the sea there is a belt of white sand called *zanderij*. The name comes from nearby Suriname, where the sands continue. The sand came from the breakdown of ancient rock, and today it covers gently sloping hills, some reaching as much as 400 feet (122 m) high. In recent geological times these sand beds have been covered with dense tropical forests made up of trees suited to the soil and climate. They are among Guyana's great resources.

Not only are the sands a source of tropical woods, but they yield bauxite, the ore from which aluminium is mined.

Today, the zanderij is covered by thick tropical forests.

The Plateau

Much of the central part of Guyana is built on a low plateau of crystalline rocks, above which stand other flat plains, such as the Kaieteurian Plateau. This tableland rises to 1,968 feet (600 m) above sea level. From it plunges the spectacular Kaieteur Falls, one of South America's greatest natural wonders.

Few places on earth can be as eerily spectacular as the Pakaraima Mountains, which dominate the western side of Guyana. If Kaieteur Falls are the opening to the drama, then the Pakaraima are all the acts in one. Kaieteur Falls can be found in the lower levels of these mountains—which rise through forests to the extraordinary Roraima tableland. From the cockpit of a tiny aircraft, sheer cliffs seem to drop for thousands of feet. Their tops are in clouds and their feet are in tropical forest. Waterfalls cascade from crevices. A closer inspection of the table surface is frightening, as landing there would be impossible. Deep cracks appear to be bottomless,

Waterfalls cascade down the Pakaraima Mountains.

Kaieteur Falls

Unlike some of the world's largest falls, the Kaieteur Falls have remained isolated in untouched forest. They are visited by only a handful of tourists who have the courage to make the one-hour flight in a small aircraft from Georgetown to a landing field on the plateau top.

The falls are on the Potaro River. At the rim they are 350 feet (107 m) wide, and the single fall over the sheer side of the plateau into a rock- and forest-filled gorge drops 741 feet (226 m). In the spray-filled gorge below, the Potaro continues over more falls and rapids, descending another 81 feet (25 m) to reach the western bank of the Essequibo River.

The falls were discovered on April 29, 1870, by C. Barrington-Brown, an English geologist and surveyor who was mapping the Potaro River. The area around the falls was declared a national park in 1930. This has helped protect the area from development, but there are plans for using the river to generate hydroelectric power.

pools of water fill hollows, and mushroom-shaped stones of eroded rock stand like sentinels. This is truly a lost world. Very few people reach the summit of Roraima from the Guyana side.

The Roraima plateau lies across the border between Guyana and Venezuela. The plateau is the highest point in Guyana at 2,835 feet (864 m) high. The summit of the mountain is in Venezuela at 2,875 feet (876 m) high. This is a generally accepted fact, though the exact route of the border between the two countries, in this wild region, is not. It is a dispute that has rumbled on for more than a century.

Guyana's Geographical Features

Area: 83,000 square miles (214,953 sq km)

Highest elevation: Plateau of Mount Roraima, 2,835 feet (864 m)

Lowest elevation: Sea level

Longest rivers: Essequibo, 630 miles (1,014 km) from south to north; Demerara, 215 miles (346 km)

Highest waterfall: Kaieteur Falls, with a drop of 741 feet (226 m)

Longest shared border: 695 miles (1,118 km) with Brazil

Annual average rainfall: 90 inches (229 cm) along the coast; 70 inches (178 cm) inland

Annual average temperature: 79°F (26°C) in January in Georgetown; 81°F (27°C) in July in Georgetown

Coastline: 285 miles (459 km)

Greatest distance north to south: 495 miles (797 km)

Greatest distance east to west: 290 miles (467 km)

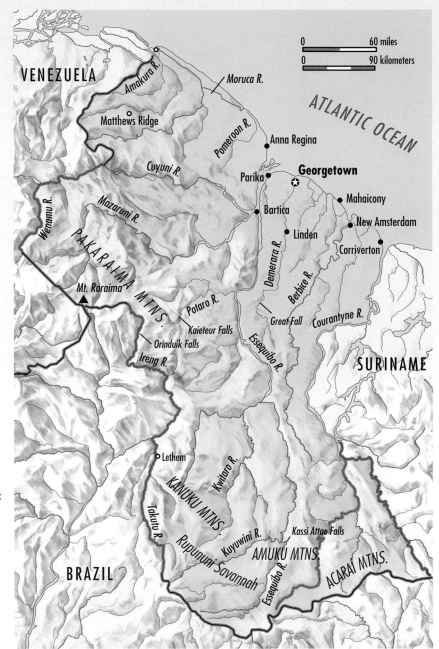

The Pakaraima Mountains form the meeting point for Guyana, Venezuela, and Brazil. Water draining to Guyana eventually enters the Essequibo River. Rivers starting on the Brazilian side flow to the Amazon River and those in Venezuela head for the Orinoco River. Other, lower mountains, the Kanuku, lie to the south of the Pakaraima. In the far south are the Kamoa and Amuku Mountains, and the Acaraí, which straddle part of Guyana's border with Brazil.

Broad Savannas and Ancient Lakes

At their southern end, the Pakaraima Mountains end abruptly. Within a very short distance of each other, several high points reach about 3,000 feet (914 m). Then, suddenly, the land drops to just one-tenth of the altitude and opens to fine savanna

Low-lying grasslands of the savanna

Ancient Lake Parima is now
the Rupununi Savanna.

country with open grasslands and in places, a scattering of stunted trees.

The town of Lethem lies on the southwest side of the Guyana savanna. It borders Brazil beside the river Takutu, an Amazon tributary. A poor road leads northeast from Lethem, crossing streams that flow into the Rupununi River, a tributary of the Essequibo. The streams almost form a link between the two great water systems of the Essequibo and the Amazon.

Around the time of the last Ice Age, some 25,000 years ago, this part of Guyana was covered by a shallow lake called Lake Parima. Today, the ancient bed of the lake stretches as flat as a football field to the Essequibo River. It is known as the Rupununi, or the Rupununi Savanna. Remnants of Lake Parima, such as the small Lake Amuku, still exist. Sometimes, when Amuku floods in the rainy seasons, the water extends without interruption to the horizon. This is much as how Lake Parima is depicted on 300-year-old maps. According to early explorers, Lake Parima was on the route to El Dorado.

Rivers Are Like That

There is something about a river that fires the imagination. White waters are exciting and full of adventure. The calm places are soothing and loved by fishers. The Amerindians of Guyana have legends, which have passed from generation to generation, about their rivers. Native American names give a clue to the past. *Aturwau* Creek means "alligator" in the Wapishana language and *Kassi Attae* Rapids get their name from a catfish known as Kassi. The Kuyuwini, another river, tells of the wildlife. It is named after *cuyu*, which in the Wapishana language is the word for the white-headed guam, a game bird, and *wini*, which is "water." *Shawtarli* means "eagle rock" for the Waiwai, another tribe, while the *Ramarawau* River is "Hair-oil River" in Wapishana. *Amuku* in Makushi means "old man," perhaps relating it to Lake Parima and the tales of that ancient lake.

Jungle Peace

"A PLACE MORE WONDERFUL THAN ANY FAIRY LAND of which I have read." So wrote the American naturalist William Beebe about his travels to Guyana early in the last century. Beebe was a longtime director of tropical research at the New York Zoological Society (Bronx Zoo). Guyana— then British Guiana—became his passion and his wilderness laboratory.

Opposite: **Jaguars are the largest cats found in the jungles of Guyana.**

An Adventure in Guyana

Charles William Beebe, one of the most famous American naturalists, was born in Brooklyn, New York, in 1877 and grew up in New Jersey. A formal education led him to natural history, and his skill as a writer and enthusiasm for birds took him all over the world. One of his earliest adventures was in 1909 when, with his wife, Mary, he set out from New York on a Dutch steamship bound for Georgetown. It took a week to get there. They had planned to head for the Essequibo River but changed their route to a journey into the northwestern forest close to the Venezuelan border. Beebe's account, written with Mary, is filled with the excitement of a search. They found snakes galore, including the giant anaconda, which grows to almost 30 feet (9 m); many birds, including toucans, tiny hummingbirds, and the magnificent orange cock-of-the-rock (below); strange mammals like vampire bats; and legions of insects.

Fertile Forests

Guyana's tropical forests are one of the finest reserves in the world. Together with forests in Suriname and French Guiana, the region has every chance of remaining comparatively untouched for a long time. Of the three countries, there is greater impact from development in Guyana. Even so, huge parts of the interior are untouched. Fine woods are plentiful. Logging has not had the same devastating effect as in neighboring Brazil.

The vibrant tabebuia

One of the most striking trees of the interior is the yellow flowering tabebuia. It has a fine, hard wood, and at one time was sought after for making bows. Moras are trees of the zanderij forest. They have been called the oaks of the tropics because their wood was used for boatbuilding; today it is used for buildings. These trees can reach as much as 200 feet (more than 60 m) high, though 120 feet (37 m) is normal. They have large supporting buttresses, or flanges, starting at ground level. The trunks, which are about 3 feet (almost 1 m) across, rear upward for 60 feet (more than 18 m) before the branches spread.

Moriche palms are an important resource.

A South American bromeliad

Apart from these striking trees there are dozens more species, including palms, such as the moriche, that grow at the edges of rivers and in the coastal strip. The moriche palm produces nearly everything anyone could need. Its fibers make thread, its wood is excellent for housing, its leaves are good thatch, and its sap is used as a drink.

The forest contains many other plants. Bromeliads are relatives of pineapples. They are uniquely tropical American plants that grow on branches, on the ground, on rocks, and at the water's edge. Some, like the aechmeas, have showy flowers, while others are tiny. Lichens, mosses, and fungi abound on old trees and on the forest floor, which is damp and forbidding. Turn over a stump and a wealth of life begins to move. Spiders, centipedes, and insects of all kinds scurry for the nearest darkness.

A Jungle Pharmacy

William Beebe was not the first naturalist to be entranced by Guyana, and certainly not the last. Beginning in 1812, Charles Waterton, an eccentric Englishman, made four journeys to Guyana. His classic book *Wanderings in South America* is filled with carefully drawn illustrations and descriptive notes about the wildlife and native peoples. One of Waterton's first quests was for *curare*, the poison used by some forest tribes on their blowgun darts and arrow tips.

Guyana, with its extensive forests, contains many of the remedies taken for granted in modern medicine. The curare sought by Waterton is now made in factories and used in surgery. In his day, and to some extent even now, curare is made by forest Amerindians by taking the sap from certain vines, slender plants that trail from others in the forest. First they scrape the bark off the vine and add it to cold water. Then they add some thirty other ingredients. The full process is a closely guarded secret.

The deadly curare relaxes muscles. Monkeys stay well out of reach of the poison darts by using their tails to hang firmly on branches in the tall trees. If they are hit with a curare dart, their muscles relax and they simply let go. The forests of the Kanuku mountain range have many vines of the type needed to make curare.

Many Monkeys

Guyana's forests are home to many South American monkeys, but the one most likely to be noticed is the howler. Howlers

Howler monkeys calling out from the treetops

are not seen very often, but they are heard. Their booming call echoes through the trees at dawn and dusk. The sound comes from their throats, where one of the bones is especially enlarged, thin, and hollow. The sound is difficult to describe as it resembles a strong, vibrating wind rushing through the trees.

Tamarins are some of the smallest primates in the forests—usually not much more than 6 to 8 inches (15 to 20 cm) high with tails of the same length or longer. The red-handed tamarin is almost black, and its front limbs have reddish gold hands. These tiny animals, which live in pairs, feed on flowers, fruits, insects, snails, and various small reptiles.

The Hoatzin

Sometimes called the "stinking bird" for its musky smell, the hoatzin, or Canje pheasant, is one of South America's most unusual animals. It is Guyana's national bird, distantly related to pheasants. In size it is about 2 feet (61 cm) long from head to tail. The color is dark brown above and lighter, reddish yellow below. The head is small, with bare blue skin around the eyes, and crowned with a bristling array of short feathers. But there ends the simple story.

The young birds have wings armed with moveable claws, and they climb around the riverside bushes near their nest. If there is danger about, the chicks drop into the water, where they can dive, swim, and climb out. The claws, which are lost at adulthood, may be remnants from an earlier bird that was far closer to a reptilean ancestor. As adults, hoatzins are poor fliers because they have weak flight muscles, and the best they can manage is an ungainly powered glide. Up to fifty birds live in a colony. They are often difficult to see, but the sound of them flapping about in the bushes gives away their location.

Forests grow right to the water's edge, often with branches hanging low over the water. In the high-water season some branches may become submerged. All around at water level there is an impenetrable tangle of vines and other plants. Hoatzins can be found here, feeding on the fruit, leaves, and flowers of two plants, the white mangrove and a giant relative of the ornamnental houseplant monstera.

The National Flower: Queen Victoria's Lily

The giant water lily *Victoria amazonica* (or *regia*) has floating, circular leaves of up to 6.5 feet (2 m) across. It was named in honor of the British monarch Queen Victoria (1819–1901). Explorer Robert Schomburgk discovered it in 1835 when he was exploring the British colony. Later, his brother Richard wrote that in the Rupununi they gazed on the plants in "silent wonder." The *Victoria amazonica* is Guyana's national flower.

The edge of the leaf is turned up by several inches, making it appear like a shallow pan. There is a legend that the largest leaves will support the weight of a small child. Certainly frogs and other small animals can sit on the leaves without any problem. The flowers are about 12 inches (30 cm) across, with the outer petals white and inner ones deep purple to rose. The botanical garden in Georgetown has a canal filled with the lilies, and many natural lagoons in the interior are filled edge to edge with the plants.

Black Rivers

Rivers flowing from the ancient rocky plateaus are called black rivers. Their water is the color of rich, clear tea and has very little mud. The Potaro River is like this. The Kaieteur Falls glisten a transparent brown. The color is due to a stain from decaying forest floor vegetation drained by streams. Some rivers, such as those in the northwest, are muddier.

In places where there are rapids, many of the rocks are covered with the unusual podestemon plants, of which there are many species. Without water or spray covering them, they soon die. The most obvious are those that are flowering, but they flower for only a short time.

Big Fish, Little Fish

Guyana's rivers abound with many kinds of fish. One of the smallest is the unusual four-eyed anableps. It appears to have

Anableps's eyes allow them to see above and below the water.

four eyes, but really has just two. This fish often swims near the surface with its eyes half-protruding. The apparently divided lens allows for a different focus above and below water. The payara is a fierce looking carnivorous fish that is about 3 feet (90 cm) long and has massive fanglike teeth.

With so many rivers and creeks, the Amerindians have caught fish for centuries. Rather than using lines, they prefer to use a poison pressed from a forest vine. For a riverside family, it is a simple task to beat some lengths of the vine with stones and then throw the poison into pools where the fish gather. Soon the fish are belly-up on the surface but still perfectly safe to eat. Unfortunately, the poison has been exploited commercially and sometimes used in excessive amounts, killing fish for miles downriver.

A different kind of fishing technique is needed to bag an arapaima, which has been said to reach 15 feet (4.6 m). It is the longest of Guyana's freshwater fishes. Usually the arapaima is much smaller, as they are now fished commercially for food.

Out for an Arapaima

Tiny McTurk's British ancestors arrived in Guyana more than 150 years ago. He founded the Karambo ranch in the 1920s. A legendary backwoodsman, he would catch arapaima in a creek near the ranch. Working from a canoe, Tiny first made floats from pieces of dry branch. Each float had a stout line and a 9-inch (23-cm) hook that he baited with pieces of freshly caught fish, often a piranha or cannibal fish. Once several of the baited lines were over the side, he watched until one bobbed down in the water. Then he would grab the float and pull. Sometimes the fish escaped, though more often than not there was an enormous struggle as Tiny pulled it to the canoe. Then, using an iron-tipped pole, he harpooned it in the side. A large arapaima took two men to haul aboard. Dried in the sun, the meat fed several families for several weeks.

A giant river otter

Untamed Animals

Many of Guyana's animals are similar to those of other northern South America areas. The jaguar is the biggest of the cats. Jaguars mostly hunt at night but are sometimes seen during the day sunning themselves on an open bank or log. Smaller carnivores are ocelots and margays. In the rivers there are otters, including the giant otter, which can reach almost 7 feet (2.1 m) long. The forest edge and savanna are home for anteaters, curiosities of the earliest South American mammals. The largest is the giant anteater, known locally as the ant bear. It is armed with powerful front limbs and claws especially adapted for tearing at termite nests, which stand like small towers in the grasslands. A smaller anteater, the tamandua, also with a long snout perfect for gathering ants, can climb trees. Even smaller is the silky anteater at only 15 inches (38 cm) long. It is covered with golden down or buff hair that is perfect camouflage among the dappled sunlight of the higher branches.

On Top of the Lost World

In the beginning, the explorers had no idea what was there. The tabletop plateau of Roraima was another world, perhaps known to the Amerindians. Perhaps not. It is quite difficult to climb up the sides, and the only routes to the summit follow deep clefts in the sandstone. The first recorded climb was in 1884. Since then, the plants and animals that live there have been studied thoroughly by specialists who now get lifted in by helicopter.

So what have the specialists found? Certainly none of Professor Challenger's monsters, but plenty of scientific curiosities. The plateau is like an island and has many plants and some birds that are only found there. In this wonderland of lost worlds, another tableland 50 miles (80 km) away has similar plants but different species. Even more exciting for the botanist is that some of the plants are part of a relic flora—unchanged for tens of thousands of years.

A sea turtle comes ashore to lay her eggs.

Back at sea level, the animal world looks back to tales from recent history. The rivers near the coast are home to the manatee, or sea cow, the mermaid of seafarers' legends. The manatees of Guyana are the same as those found in North America and browse on the underwater vegetation. Also known to the early mariners and Amerindians, who took them for food, are the marine turtles. Four species visit the northern beaches of Guyana, where they come ashore at night to lay their eggs. Their battle for survival against the natural elements is constant, and now, more than ever, they need help to survive.

Safeguarding the Future

One of South America's most ambitious rain forest protection projects was launched in 1989. About 2 percent of Guyana's rain forest was put aside in a single area to be protected and used as a biological resource.

Iwokrama Rain Forest Preserve lies on the western side of the Essequibo River near Kuratoka Falls. It takes its name from a low range of the Pakaraima Mountains that, at 3,369 feet (1,027 m), are the highest point in the reserve. Iwokrama is an Amerindian word meaning "place of refuge." It comes from a Makushi legend that says the mountains were a hiding place for part of the tribe who had been defeated in battle.

Plans for the refuge include studying the plants known to the Makushi and carefully recording all their uses, especially as food and medicines. As well as becoming a scientific center for the world community, part of the area will be set aside for sustainable production of forest products.

The Wild Coast

THE ORIGINAL PEOPLES OF GUYANA WERE TRIBES OF Amerindians who probably arrived in the region between 2,000 and 3,000 years ago. They included the Carib, Arawak, Akawaio, and Warrau tribes. Their ancestors had made their way from Asia to America some 30,000 years earlier, during the last Ice Age.

The Amerindians led simple, primitive lives, hunting and fishing. In time, they made clearings in the forest so they could grow manioc, or cassava, a root vegetable that provided their basic food and drink. They built shelters of palm thatch in the forest or lived on the banks of the rivers in cane-and-thatch huts raised on stilts. They had no need of clothing in the hot, wet tropics. Instead, they decorated their bodies with vegetable dyes.

From the end of the fifteenth century, European explorers were looking for sea routes to an area of Asia then known as the Indies, what we call India and other Far East countries. Traders knew the Indies were rich in spices and silk, and they wanted an alternative to the long overland route. Christopher Columbus set out west from Spain to find

Opposite: **Original tribesmen hunted on the savanna.**

Illustration of thatch huts

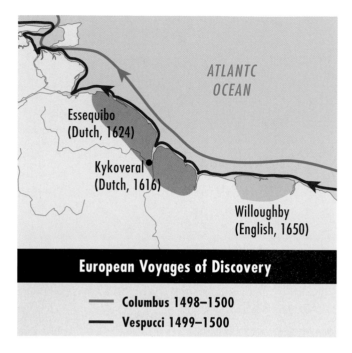

ATLANTC OCEAN

Essequibo (Dutch, 1624)

Kykoveral (Dutch, 1616)

Willoughby (English, 1650)

European Voyages of Discovery

— Columbus 1498–1500
— Vespucci 1499–1500

the Indies. His first landfall was the Bahamas in 1492. It seems likely that he sighted the coast of the Guianas on his third voyage, in 1498. At that time, the name *Guiana* was given to the present-day countries of French Guiana, Suriname, Guyana, and part of Venezuela. The Guiana coast stretched from the Orinoco River to the mouth of the Amazon.

The first European explorer to land on the northern coast of South America was Spanish captain Alonso

Sir Walter Raleigh

Most explorers arrived in the New World in search of gold and riches. They soon heard of the legendary golden king El Dorado and his golden city of Manoa. Perhaps the most famous expedition was led by British sailor, poet, historian, and explorer Sir Walter Raleigh (pictured) in 1595. He described his adventures in his book *The Discovery of the Rich and Beautiful Empire of Guiana*. He did not find the golden city, but he fell in love with the country.

Two of his captains followed in his footsteps. Lawrence Keymis was the first Englishman to explore the length of the Guiana coast. The second officer, Leonard Berry, made an unsuccessful attempt to sail up the Courantyne River. In 1617 Raleigh organized a return expedition to find a gold mine that Keymis had been told of in 1595. However, the expedition went

badly. Raleigh was sick, and his son died during a fight with Spaniards at a fort on the Orinoco River. They did not find a gold mine. On his return to England, Raleigh was executed on the grounds of treason, an old accusation based on prior acts.

de Ojeda, one of Columbus's mapmakers, in 1499. However, for a long time explorers ignored the wild Guiana lands. Not only were the deep swamps and thick forests difficult to explore, but also the explorers did not know what to expect from the Amerindians. It was one of the last areas in South America to be colonized by Europeans. The Spaniards tried unsuccessfully with an expedition in 1530. It was another thirty years before the Dutch began trading with the Amerindians.

European Settlers

By the end of the sixteenth century, the Dutch had established a profitable trade in tobacco and natural dyes from Guyana. In Europe the dyes were valued for coloring cloth and other items. The Dutch also knew of Raleigh's book and continued to search for the golden city and gold mines.

The first Dutch settlement and trading post was founded in 1616. It was called *Kykoveral*, meaning "looks over all." It was

Wealthy Dutch sugar planters established successful plantations in Guyana.

at the junction of the rivers Essequibo, Cuyuni, and Mazaruni. In 1621 the Dutch created the West India Company. This company had the only authority to trade with the Amerindians. The Dutch established a second trading post on the Berbice River.

Around the middle of the seventeenth century, Dutch sugar planters arrived and settled on the Pomeroon and Moruca Rivers. They had been forced out of neighboring Brazil by Portuguese settlers. They brought to Guiana skills they had learned from the Portuguese in cultivating and manufacturing sugar. The sugar plantations were soon more successful and prosperous than the trading stations.

British attempts to establish themselves in Guiana did not succeed until 1650, when a group of colonists led by Francis William Willoughby settled on the Suriname River. They realized that the most fertile soil was near the coast and began to develop sugar plantations around the mouth of the river. The Dutch followed them there.

During the next hundred years, all the settlements changed hands with astonishing frequency. The Dutch, French, and English were almost constantly at war in Europe and other parts of the world. The settlements became pawns in the wars, and each attacked the other many times. The colonies also suffered from raids by pirates or buccaneers, lawless men who were often escaped criminals. The fighting caused a lot of destruction, but most of the settlements survived. By the end of the eighteenth century, the region was producing sugar, coffee, cotton, and cocoa.

Draining the Land

Coastal plantations were not problem-free. Being lower than the level of the sea, they flooded easily and often. Water also drained down into the plantations from the land behind. The Dutch were used to similar conditions in Holland. They used dams and a seawall to keep the water out, and dug trenches to drain excess water from the land. They also devised a way of retaining some water for use in periods of drought. The improvements worked well, but they were expensive. Only wealthy planters could afford them. In time, the planters and their heirs became a powerful elite with a great deal of control over the colony.

Master 's-Gravesande

Laurens Storm van 's-Gravesande was the most famous Dutch commander of his time. He was in Guiana from 1738 to 1772. He was kind to the Amerindians, and they trusted him. He encouraged planters to move to the coast and develop new drainage systems. Most of all, he foresaw the importance of the Demerara River and the potential of the nearby coastal area. He autho- rized the watchtower built in 1748 at the mouth of the river that is the site of present-day Georgetown. By the time 's-Gravesande left Guiana, Demerara was the most important settlement. He was also responsible for the settlement's first form of government, called a Council of Policy; there was also a court of law called a Council of Justice.

The English Take Over

There were probably more English settlers in Guiana by the mid-1700s than any other nationality. But events taking place in the rest of the world meant that the future of the colonies remained unsettled for many years. France and England were at war from 1756 to 1763, and the American War of Independence followed in 1775. England believed the Dutch were supporting the colonists in America and retaliated by attacking Dutch colonies. In 1781 the English took Demerara, Essequibo, and Berbice, gaining control of the Dutch settlements.

One year later, all three settlements were taken by the French. But France was forced to hand them back to Holland at the Treaty of Versailles two years later. In the short time they were there, the French

British troops occupying Guyana

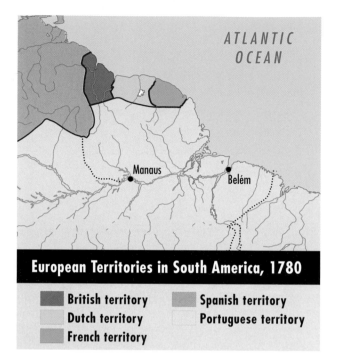

developed a new, small town around the watchtower at the mouth of the Demerara, calling it Longchamps. The Dutch carried on the work, though changing the name to Stabroek.

At the end of the eighteenth century, events in Europe continued to dictate the future of Guiana. Alliances made at the end of the French Revolution (1789) led to the Dutch giving up the colonies once again to England. Planters and colonists arrived from England in good number. They bought land and invested in cotton, sugar, and coffee. There was hope and prosperity. But when peace returned to Europe in 1802, the colonies were once again given back to Holland. This time the English planters were very angry.

The planters did not have to wait long for the English to take over. The next year they were back—this time for good. In the next few years Guiana became wealthier through its exports. The authorities encouraged the use of the English language rather than Dutch. Englishmen were appointed to official positions and took part in local politics. Stabroek grew dramatically and was renamed George Town in 1812, after King George III. (In 1841 the name became Georgetown.)

Meanwhile, Emperor Napoléon Bonaparte was finally defeated in France in 1814 and forced to make peace. As part of the peace agreements, Britain paid Holland for the three settlements in Guiana. They would remain under British rule until independence in 1966.

Slavery

When the sugar plantations were started, there was a shortage of workers in Guiana. The Amerindians were not up to the strict hard labor. So the planters brought black slaves from Africa. The Dutch West India Company was already trading there. Ships took cheap manufactured goods from Europe to Africa; there they were sold or exchanged for slaves. Then the slaves were transported to the New World. The ships would also take on board a cargo of sugar, tobacco, and other items for the journey homeward to Europe.

The first shipload of slaves arrived in 1658. Tens of thousands of black captives followed. Their lives were a misery.

Slaves worked on plantations under the watchful eyes of their master.

Slaves were made to work long hours, given little food, and whipped if they made mistakes or were disobedient. Families were split up. Many tried to run away, but they risked being caught by the Amerindians. The plantations could not survive without the slaves, and owners dealt severely with any kind of trouble.

The Berbice Rebellion

In 1763 there was a slave rebellion in Berbice. The settlers ran for their lives wherever they could—into the bush, onto boats at sea. Many were killed and their weapons seized. The slaves won the first round and pushed on to take nearby Fort Nassau, where many of the settlers and the governor of Berbice had taken refuge. But there was jealousy and resentment among the slaves, mainly because they came from different African tribal backgrounds. Also, many did not trust the leader, Cuffy. The delay allowed the governor and his people to escape from the fort. One African leader, Akara, decided to lead an attack on the governor, but he failed. When Cuffy eventually led the main attack, he too was repulsed by the governor's forces. The rebellion was crushed. Cuffy took his own life, and today is regarded as a hero. A statue in Georgetown (photo) honors Cuffy and the Africans who died.

The British government abolished the trading of slaves in 1807, though not the holding of slaves. Some years later, a misunderstanding of the English law led slaves on a plantation on the east coast of Demerara to stop working. They believed the king of England had granted them the right to be free and that the European planters were withholding that right from them. They took the European managers and overseers captive. They did, though, treat the Europeans quite well and leniently. This was in large part due to the influence of two men, Jack Gladstone and his father, Quamina, who had been converted to Christianity by missionaries working on the plantation. But the strike spread to other plantations in Demerara, and British troops were called in. They brought the rebellion to a brutal end, killing many of the slaves. Despite having risked their lives by encouraging leniency toward the Europeans, Gladstone was arrested and hanged, while Quamina was shot by an Amerindian.

British Guiana

In 1831 Demerara, Berbice, and Essequibo became the colony of British Guiana. The Emancipation Act in 1838 finally freed the slaves. They had the choice of remaining on the plantations, where they could earn wages and occupy their own homes, or they could buy their own plots of land. Some got together, pooled their resources, and bought abandoned land that they turned into villages. About half of the estimated 80,000 Afro-Guianese, or black, population settled on the coast. Often, however, they were still treated badly.

With slavery abolished, the British had to look elsewhere for workers, and they brought them from Germany, Portugal, India, and China. Small numbers of Irish, English, and Scots also came. The significance of the European workers was that they were white. The authorities hoped their numbers would balance the largely black population. The Chinese first arrived in 1853 but never in large numbers.

Immigrants from India arrived almost every year until 1917. Like the others, they were indentured, or contracted, laborers, tied to a master for a specified number of years. At times they were treated very badly, but it was difficult to escape the terms of the contract. However, once their time was up, many opted to receive land instead of a passage back to India. They remained in British Guiana, where some began to cultivate rice.

The year 1848 was eventful. There was a serious general strike by workers on the sugar plantations, opposing the conditions imposed by the planters. Two major fires destroyed all the wooden buildings on Water Street in Georgetown. A railroad was opened, the first of its kind in South America, which ran from Georgetown to the east coast of the Demerara River.

Settlement proceeded slowly during the last half of the nineteenth century. The sugar industry was not doing well because of competition from sugar-beet production in Europe. But gold was discovered in the 1880s in the northwest.

Georgetown opened a new water distribution system, and the first electric lights were switched on in January 1891. Also in that year, the first cable contact with London and New York was established, so telegrams could be exchanged.

Politically there were also some small but significant changes. The wealthy elite whose families owned the coastal plantations still controlled much of what went on in the colony. In the 1890s, some modest reforms were introduced that gave more power to locally elected officials. People began to talk about an elected house of assembly.

Road to Independence

By the beginning of the twentieth century, the Afro-Guianese were making it clear they wanted a greater say in running the country. Some had received a good education and qualified as doctors, lawyers, and teachers. Others were successful merchants

Boundary Dispute

Sir Robert Hermann Schomburgk was an explorer sent by the Royal Geographical Society of London to Guiana in 1835. He discovered both the source of the Essequibo River and, in 1838, Mount Roraima. In 1840 he was appointed by the British government to make surveys of and suggest boundaries between Guiana and Venezuela, and Guiana and Brazil. The boundary line he chose became known as the Schomburgk Line.

Toward the end of the nineteenth century, a conflict arose over the boundary between British Guiana and Venezuela. The disputed area, known as the North West District, was where most of the gold had been discovered. The United States backed Venezuela's claim, but in 1899 a tribunal awarded most of the area to British Guiana. The dispute was reopened by Venezuela when British Guiana became independent in 1966. It has still not been resolved.

and traders. Some had even been elected to the Combined Court that had the responsibility for raising taxes. There was not much the established Afro-Guianese could do for the majority of blacks, who were very poor, but one step forward was the opening of middle schools. Here, Afro-Guianese pupils received the same level of education as the better-off Guianese. This helped them qualify for better jobs, especially in government.

The wealthy planters, though, were against such improvements. They needed black labor on the plantations, and their aim was to do everything to ensure that the sugar industry remain profitable. It gave them power and prosperity. The planters did not encourage new industries, not even in gold and diamonds when large deposits of the minerals were found. When bauxite was discovered in 1914, it was companies from Canada and the United States that developed the industry, not the planters.

The planters were still very dependent on the East Indians as a workforce. The East Indians were not yet part of Guianese society. Their religious beliefs, as Hindus or Muslims, kept them apart and prevented them from sending children to the Christian schools. Few, perhaps only a third, of the immigrants had any schooling. However, those East Indians who had acquired land and cultivated rice now owned a successful industry.

Toward the end of the nineteenth century and early in the twentieth, there were many strikes and demonstrations in both rural and urban areas of Guiana. The strikers were mainly blacks, with some East Indians. They demanded better wages and wanted improved living and working conditions. The most serious strike was in 1905 by dockworkers and other workers in Georgetown. They were protesting several bad practices, including having to work ten-and-a-half hours every day, with no payment for working overtime. The strikers received good support, and the protest spread to some rural plantations. It became so serious that riots broke out and the police were called in. Several people were killed or wounded.

The strikes continued until 1916. World War I contributed some to improving wages because sugar and rice were in high demand. But after the war, wages fell. The British Guiana Labour Union, the first trade union, was formed in 1919.

Crown Colony

In 1928 British Guiana was made a British crown colony. This meant that it had a governor appointed by the British government and a Legislative Council that made the laws. The council consisted of the governor, a colonial secretary, an attorney general, and thirteen officials—all appointed. There were just fourteen elected members.

It was not a system the Guianese wanted because it gave them less power to make their own decisions. The appointed officials could outvote the elected members at any time. The British government decided it was right for the colony mainly for two reasons. Economically, the colony was depressed. If Guiana needed to borrow money and reorganize its budget, the British government felt that the British should have financial control. Also, since the turn of the century the white planters had lost much of their influence over the blacks. A crown colony could reverse this situation.

Strikes continued throughout the 1930s, and people were killed. The situation was so bad that the British arranged for a report on the situation. The report recommended, among other things, that many more people be given the right to vote. During the 1950s, political activity increased. The constitution was reformed. General elections were held in 1953 in which everyone over twenty-one who was literate could vote.

Politicians of the People's Progressive Party

Political parties were formed, and two politicians emerged who would dominate Guianese politics until almost the end of the century. They were Dr. Cheddi Jagan and Forbes Burnham.

Together they formed the People's Progressive Party (PPP) and easily won the 1953 elections with a majority of seats in the House of Assembly. Jagan became the country's prime minister. He introduced radical social and economic reforms. Demonstrations and strikes by workers were encouraged by his party. This angered the British authorities. They dismissed him from office, suspended the constitution, and sent in troops because they believed that Jagan and the PPP were trying to turn Guiana into a communist state.

The PPP divided in 1955. Jagan continued as leader of the PPP, predominately an East Indian party, and Burnham led a party, principally of Afro-Guianese, called the People's National Congress (PNC). The racial divide between the two parties came to dominate Guianese politics for more than forty years and often led to violent tensions.

The British restored the constitution in 1957. Elections held that year and again in 1961 were won by Jagan. He

Cheddi Jagan attends his victory parade in August 1961.

remained committed to his socialist programs, a situation that did not please either the British or the U.S. governments, who worked to undermine his position. Over the next four years there were riots, strikes, looting, and burning of buildings.

By 1960 independence for British Guiana was high on the Crown Colony's agenda. At a conference in London in 1963, the British government agreed to grant independence to the colony. But there was a condition: First there would be another election, in which proportional representation would be introduced. This is a different way of counting votes that favors smaller parties. It was widely believed that this system would reduce the number of votes for the PPP and increase those for the PNC, which the British and U.S. governments favored. In the elections, the PPP gained most votes, but a coalition between the PNC and a third party gave Burnham the majority. He became the first prime minister of the newly independent nation in May 1966.

Cooperative Republic

With independence, British Guiana changed its name to Guyana. Four years later, in 1970, it became the Cooperative Republic of Guyana. By becoming a republic, it cut off the last ties with the British monarchy, although it remained a member of the British Commonwealth of Nations.

During the 1970s Guyana moved toward becoming a socialist nation. Forbes Burnham nationalized foreign companies such as those running the bauxite and sugar industries. Soon the government owned more than three-quarters of the

Guyana suffered under the leadership of Forbes Burnham.

Hugh Desmond Hoyte makes a victory sign after casting his vote.

country's production, and it controlled prices. Guyana became friendly with communist countries like the Soviet Union, East Germany, and Cuba. The government also took over all schools and promised free education from nursery school to college. The Anglican and Catholic Churches, which ran a number of schools, opposed this decision.

Burnham continued as prime minister until 1980. He was then president until his death in 1985. He was always very much in control. He relied heavily on the Guyana Defence Force, which was largely black and pro-PNC, to carry out his wishes. Elections were rigged, and he revised the constitution to give himself more power. The press was no longer free to write what it liked. His economic policies were disastrous, and corruption was widespread.

In 1985 Burnham was succeeded by Hugh Desmond Hoyte. Hoyte inherited an economy that was in trouble. He tried to resolve the problem by encouraging foreigners to invest in Guyana. He became friendly with the United States and Canada. Tourists were welcomed. By 1991 there were signs of improvement, but still not for the majority of the Guyanese. Amid more discontent, elections were held in 1992. Cheddi Jagan of the PPP won easily. The elections were declared by independent observers to be free and fair for the first time since independence.

The election gave foreigners more confidence to invest in businesses in Guyana, and Jagan continued to encourage this. He also emphasized the need for improving standards of health, housing, and education, but moved away from many of his earlier socialist ideas. He saw a modest recovery in the economy, but at the time of his death in 1997 very little had changed for the people as a whole.

New elections were held later that year. The PPP won. Jagan's wife, Janet, was installed as president. Desmond Hoyte and the PNC disputed the results. People rioted and demonstrated in the streets. Early in 1998 the two parties signed a peace deal that promised new elections and changes to the constitution. Janet Jagan resigned in 1999, and Bharrat Jagdeo of the PPP became president. New elections in March 2001 confirmed Bharrat Jagdeo as president and Samuel Hinds as prime minister.

President Bharrat Jagdeo (right) and Prime Minister Samuel Hinds

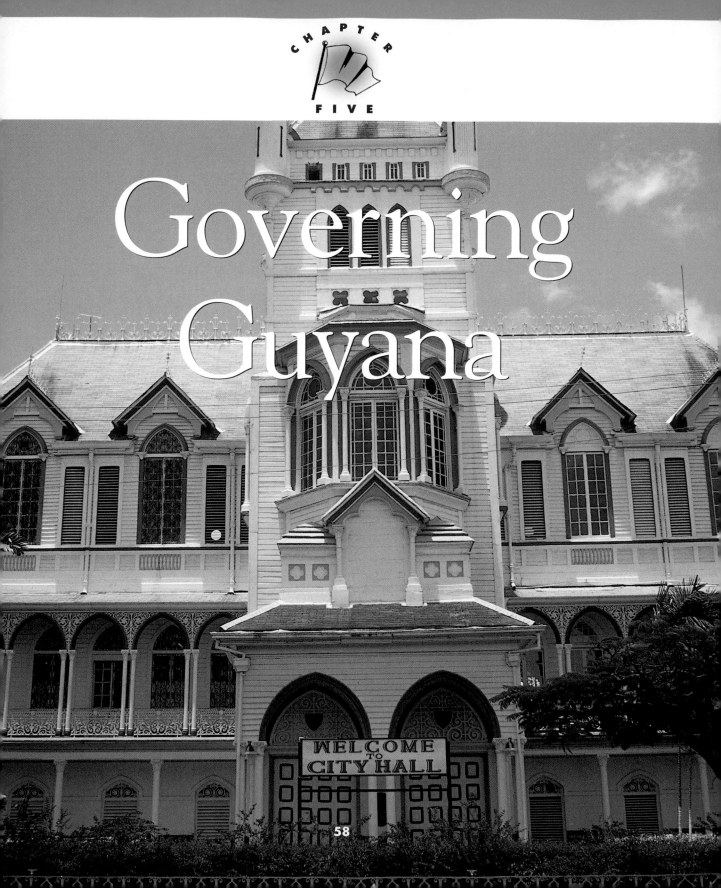

Governing
Guyana

WELCOME
TO
CITY HALL

In 1980 THE GUYANESE GOVERNMENT CHANGED THE CON-stitution to give the president executive power. This means the president is chief executive and head of state. The leader of the largest political party in the National Assembly is the person appointed president. He appoints the prime minister, who as head of government is also first vice president of the assembly; a second vice president; and a cabinet of nineteen ministers.

The responsibilities of the ministers include education, health, housing, finance, agriculture, and foreign affairs. There are also ministers of culture, youth and sports, marine resources, and Amerindian affairs. The prime minister and the cabinet are responsible to the National Assembly.

Opposite: **City Hall, Georgetown**

Prime Minister Samuel Hinds (center) in session with two of his ministers.

The Golden Arrowhead

Guyana's flag, known as the Golden Arrowhead, is made up of five colors. The green background symbolizes the forests and agricultural land. The red triangle symbolizes a bright future for an independent nation. The golden arrowhead stands for the country's mineral wealth. The black border is for the endurance of the people to ensure the country's future, and the white border is for the importance of Guyana's many rivers.

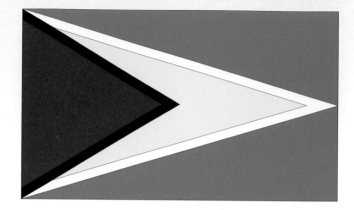

Coat of Arms

One People, One Nation, One Destiny. These are the words on Guyana's coat of arms, created when the country became independent in 1966. The design consists of an Amerindian headdress symbolizing the indigenous people of the country; two diamonds, for the mining industry; a helmet as a symbol of monarchy; and two jaguars holding a pickax, a stalk of sugarcane, and a stalk of rice symbolize workers and industry. The shield is decorated with the national flower (the *Victoria amazonica* lily) and the national bird (the hoatzin, or Canje pheasant), and three blue wavy lines represent the many waters of Guyana.

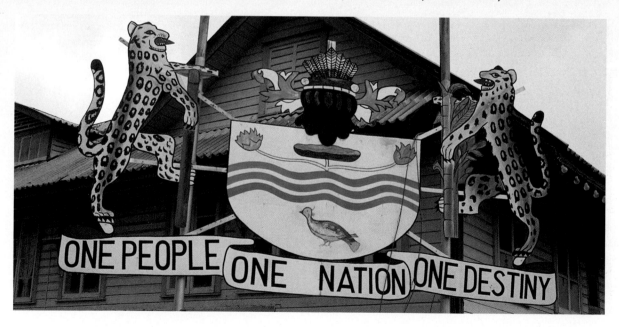

Making the Laws

Guyana's parliament is a one-house National Assembly made up of sixty-five members. Fifty-three of the members are elected by popular vote. An additional twelve members are elected by regional councils. Members hold office for five years. The leader of the opposition is elected by the minority parties in the assembly. The National Assembly is responsible for making and passing laws, although the president has the power to veto them. The parliament is housed in the Parliament Building, built in 1834.

In the Parliament Building, laws are made and passed by the National Assembly.

Keeping the Laws

The constitution is the highest law in the land. The most important court is the Supreme Court. It is made up of a High Court and the Court of Appeal. The High Court is concerned with civil and criminal matters. Criminal cases are always tried by a jury of twelve people. The Court of Appeal listens to and decides on criminal cases in which an accused person believes he or she has been wrongly convicted. Lower, or magistrate, courts in each region hear claims involving small sums of money or

Civil and criminal cases are heard in the High Court Building.

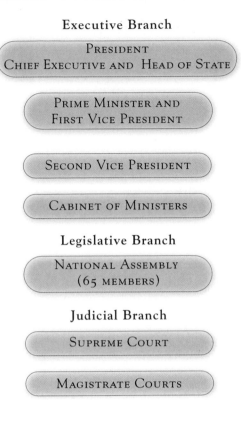

NATIONAL GOVERNMENT OF GUYANA

Executive Branch

PRESIDENT
CHIEF EXECUTIVE AND HEAD OF STATE

PRIME MINISTER AND
FIRST VICE PRESIDENT

SECOND VICE PRESIDENT

CABINET OF MINISTERS

Legislative Branch

NATIONAL ASSEMBLY
(65 MEMBERS)

Judicial Branch

SUPREME COURT

MAGISTRATE COURTS

minor offenses. The president appoints the chancellor of the High Court, the chief justice of the Court of Appeal, and the chief magistrate.

Casting a Vote

Women were given the right to vote in 1928, and now everyone over the age of eighteen can vote. Voting is carried out by secret ballot under a system of proportional representation. This means that votes are cast for candidates on voting lists

Georgetown: Did You Know This?

Population (1999 est.): 275,000

Year founded: 1781; took name of George Town in 1812; then Georgetown, 1841

Altitude: Sea level

Average daily temperature: 80°F (27°C)

Average annual rainfall: 90 inches (229 cm)

The face of modern Georgetown reflects past history. Many buildings are made from wood and the streets are named after old canals once used to drain the land. There are no tall concrete and glass structures. Houses and offices have wooden shutters to give shade from the sun. Colorful trees and grassy spaces provide freshness in the tropical climate. Names are immensely varied coming from English, such as St. George's Cathedral, Dutch as in the Stabroek Market, or from one of the diverse ethnic sources. The Jama Masjid Mosque is one and another is the Umana Yana, a large shelter built of forest materials by Amerindians for an international conference in 1972.

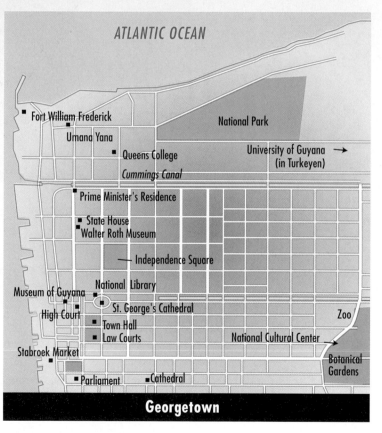

Voting lists hang at an inscription center in Georgetown.

put up by the political parties. All votes are taken into account, and seats are allocated proportionally among the lists. The system was used for the first time for the elections just before independence. It has not prevented fraud or rigging, which has affected almost every election since.

Political Parties

Eleven political parties took part in the 2001 elections:

PPP/Civic	People's Progressive Party/Civic
PNC/R	People's National Congress/Reform
GAP/WPA	Guyana Action Party/Working People's Alliance

Heads of State

Linden Forbes Sampson Burnham was born in 1923 in a village near Georgetown. He was the second son of the headmaster of a Methodist primary school. He studied law at the University of London and returned to British Guiana in 1949. At first he worked alongside Cheddi Jagan, but their political views were different. Jagan was left-wing; Burnham more moderate. They split up, and Burnham formed the People's National Congress (PNC) party. He became independent Guyana's first head of state. But then he changed course and adopted socialist policies. Under his leadership Guyana became a cooperative republic. Burnham began to act more like a dictator, and it was generally agreed that the elections that put him in power were fraudulent. However, he stayed in control, becoming president of Guyana in 1980 and ruling until his death five years later.

Cheddi Bharrat Jagan was born in 1918. He was one of eleven children of an East Indian sugar estate foreman. He qualified as a dentist in the United States and returned to British Guiana with his U.S.-born wife,

Janet (photo), in 1943. He created the country's first modern political party, the People's Progressive Party (PPP). In 1953 he became prime minister. The British authorities believed he was pro-communist and dismissed him from office. His party won the 1957 elections, and Jagan was prime minister until 1964. He was not elected to power again until 1992, when the PPP won the elections. He became president, but died in office five years later. His wife was elected president after a few months. She had been involved in politics since 1953, when she was one of the first women to be elected to the British Guiana legislature. Janet Jagan resigned on the grounds of ill health in 1999.

JFAP	Justice for All Party
ROAR	Rise, Organise, and Rebuild
TUF	The United Force
GDP	Guyana Democratic Party
NFA	National Front Alliance
NDF	National Democratic Front
GNC	Guyana National Congress
PRP	People's Republic Party

Regions

1	Barima-Waini	**6**	East Berbice-Corentyne
2	Pomeroon-Supenaam	**7**	Cuyuni-Mazaruni
3	Essequibbo Islands	**8**	Potaro-Siparuni
	West Demerara	**9**	Upper Takutu-
4	Demerara-Mahaica		Upper Essequibo
5	Mahaica-Berbice	**10**	Upper Demerara-Upper Berbice

The final count registered a clear victory for the PPP/Civic, with 209,031 votes against the PNC/R's 164,074 votes. The extent to which these two parties dominate Guyanese politics is shown in the results of the other parties. Third in the elections was GAP, with less than 10,000 votes. No other party received more than 4,000 votes, while the GNC, the NDF, and the PRP received none.

Local Government

The 1980 constitution divided Guyana into ten regions. Each region was then divided into subregions, the subregions into districts, the districts into communities, the communities into neighborhoods, and the neighborhoods into people's cooperative units.

Each region has its own Democratic Council with elected members. They stay in office for five years and four months. Local districts are governed by village or city councils.

Region 1: Barima-Waini takes its name from two rivers. Very few people live in this region. Logging is the main industry. There are some fine beaches, including Shell Beach, famous as a nesting place for turtles.

Region 2: Pomeroon-Supenaam, also known as "Rice Land" because large amounts of rice are cultivated here.

Region 3: Essequibo Islands-West Demerara is made up of islands in the Esssequibo River and part of mainland Demerara. Much of the land has been drained for cultivation.

Region 4: Demerara-Mahaica is the most populated region. It includes Georgetown; about a quarter of Guyana's people live in the capital.

Region 5: Mahaica-Berbice lies between the two rivers of the same names. Rice, sugar, and coconuts are the main crops. Amerindians of the region also make fine handicrafts.

Region 6: East Berbice-Corentyne is the second most populated region and is the only one with three towns: New Amsterdam, Rose Hall, and Corriverton.

Region 7: Cuyuni-Mazaruni is a vast area with a small population of about 15,000 people. Most of them are involved in mining for gold and diamonds.

Region 8: Potaro-Siparuni is home to the famous Kaieteur and Orinduik Falls. The very few people who live here are involved in mining and forestry.

Region 9: Upper Takutu-Upper Essequibo is known as cattle country because of its vast grasslands and large ranches. Like Region 7, it is a huge area where only about 15,000 people live in scattered villages.

Region 10: Upper Demerara-Upper Berbice is where Guyana's principal bauxite deposits are located.

"Dear Land of Guyana"

The music of the national anthem was written by R. C. G. Potter and its words are by A. L. Luker. They are written in honor of the beauty of the land and a free and united country. Here are the first and last verses:

Dear land of Guyana, of rivers and plains,
Made rich by the sunshine and lush by the rains,
Set gemlike and fair between mountains and sea,
Your children salute you, dear land of the free.

Dear land of Guyana, to you will we give
Our homage, our service, each day that we live;
God guard you, great Mother, and make us to be
More worthy of our heritage—land of the free.

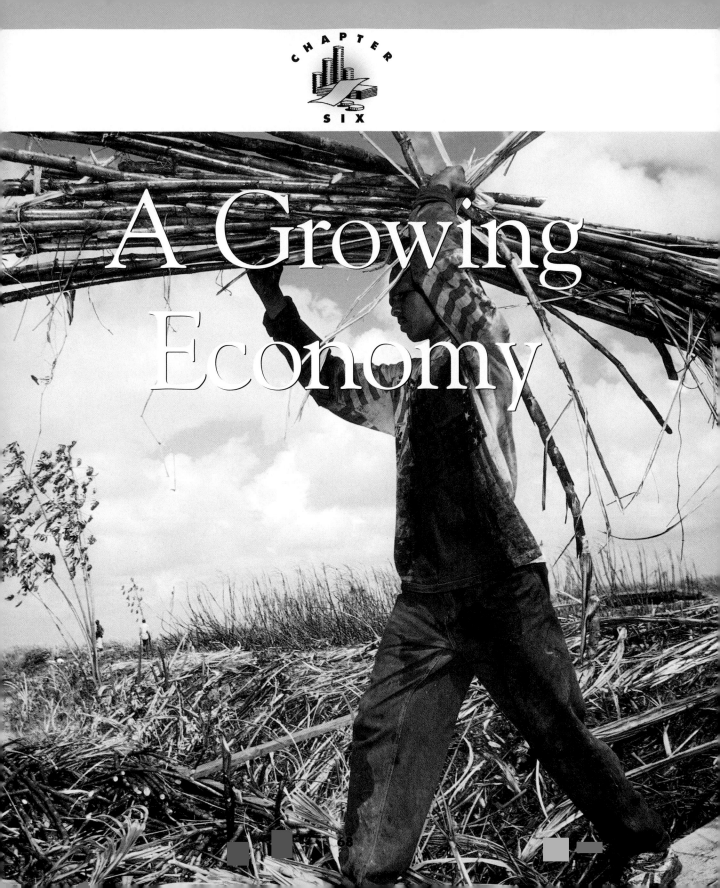

A Growing Economy

WHEN GUYANA BECAME INDEPENDENT IN 1966, MOST of the country's agricultural and mining industries belonged to overseas companies. One British company, Booker McConnell, produced 85 percent of Guyana's sugar, ran many shops and businesses, and employed 13 percent of the workforce. North American companies controlled most of the bauxite and gold-mining industries. These industries brought in about 45 percent of the money British Guiana had earned from its exports to other countries. Banks, also, were run by foreigners.

Forbes Burnham and his government believed foreign control was bad for the economy. One of their arguments was that basic resources like bauxite and sugar were being exported cheaply.

Opposite: **Cane is bundled before being loaded onto barges.**

A tractor pulling barges loaded with sugarcane

For Guyana, importing finished products like aluminium parts (for which bauxite was used) and processed foods was expensive. Why, they asked, shouldn't Guyana manufacture its own finished products and sell them to the rest of the world? During the next few years, the Guyanese government took over most of the foreign companies, and by the end of the decade it controlled more than 80 percent of the economy.

For a short time in the 1970s, industries controlled by the government seemed to work well and the economy grew. But the improvement was based largely on high world prices for bauxite and sugar. It was bad news for Guyana when these prices fell in the 1980s. The Guyanese economy also suffered because of a lack of new investment and a shortage of skilled experts and managers to run the industries. Large numbers of Guyanese had left the country after independence to look for better opportunities elsewhere. An estimated 10 percent of the population emigrated between 1976 and 1981.

At the same time, Guyana was borrowing large sums of money from international banks and organizations. The United States did not offer the same aid that it gave to other Latin American countries because it did not approve of the Guyana government's socialist policies. By 1990 Guyana owed billions of dollars to international banks and governments. At the same time, it was one of the poorest countries in the Western Hemisphere. An

Almost half of Guyanese laborers earn only 50 cents per day.

Money Facts

In 1900 the British began using British coins in British Guiana—crowns, half-crowns, florins, shillings, six-pence, three pence, pennies, and halfpennies. Instead of pounds and half-pounds, they introduced notes based on the dollar. In 1951 the British Guiana government decided to use only dollars and cents and withdrew the British coins from circulation.

Guyana's 20-dollar note has Kaieteur Falls on the front side, and the reverse features shipbuilding and the ferry vessel *Malali*. In the Guyanese Creole language, "malali" is also the nickname for the 20-dollar bill, while a 500-dollar bill is a "rag" and a 1,000-dollar bill is a "towel."

estimated 40 percent of workers earned the minimum wage, which was equal to U.S.$.50 per day. Many people depended on money sent to them by their relatives or friends overseas.

A New Policy

A change in economic policy came about only after Burnham's death in 1985, when President Hugh Desmond Hoyte launched an Economic Recovery Program. This included turning industry back into private ownership and inviting foreigners to invest again. The government cut back its spending, which made life even more difficult for the ordinary workers. They took home less pay, yet had to pay higher taxes. Desmond Hoyte had little choice but to introduce these reforms. It was the only way that international banks and governments would agree to loan Guyana the money it needed to develop the economy. The reforms proved quite successful, and the economy improved steadily for most of the 1990s.

Sugar, rice, bauxite, and gold are still the most profitable exports and account for almost 80 percent of sales to overseas markets. But new products and manufactured items are now also important. Exports now include shrimp, timber, diamonds, garments, and locally assembled stoves and refrigerators. President Bharrat Jagdeo has continued to encourage foreign investment. He has also reached an agreement with foreign banks that makes it easier for Guyana to pay back some of the billions of dollars it owes to other countries and organizations.

This worker unloads fresh shrimp that will be frozen and sent to a processing plant.

What Guyana Grows, Makes, and Mines

Agriculture (1998 est.)

Sugarcane	2,600,000 metric tons
Rice	532,000 metric tons
Coconuts	56,000 metric tons

Manufacturing

Soft drinks (1966)	4,253,000 cases
Textiles (1995)	322,000,000 meters
Foot wear (1995)	54,000 pairs

Mining (1997 est.)

Bauxite	2,467,000 metric tons
Gold	29,808 pounds (13,521 kg)

Agriculture

Sugar estates extend from the very edge of Georgetown along the coast and inland. Dotted here and there with tall palms, vast acres of green sugarcane are divided into regular-sized fields. They are crossed by the network of canals and dikes built some 300 years ago. These control the flow of water over the plantations. An important element in keeping the soil fertile is a practice called flood fallowing. Every three or four years land is flooded for at least six months before the next planting. This can be done because the land is very flat and there is a good supply of fresh water. Flooding refreshes the soil and it also helps kill weeds.

At harvestime men and women cut most of the cane by hand. This is hard work as cane grows to about twice a person's

Sugarcane is harvested by hand.

height. It is then loaded onto flat-bottomed barges that tractors or oxen pull along the canals to processing plants. During processing the pulp is separated from the cane juice. The pulp is used to make paper products and for fuel in factories and vehicles.

Demerara Sugar

Guyana produces one of the world's finest raw sugars, the golden brown Demerara sugar, which takes its name from the sugar-producing Demerara region in Guyana. It is widely used to give "that extra something" to delicious puddings and cakes. One of London's most fashionable stores offers "afternoon tea with a little strainer, a tiny metal dish to rest the strainer in, real cream, and cubes of Demerara Sugar."

Many thousands of people work in the sugar industry, which is the largest in the country. It is run by the Guyana Sugar Corporation (Guysuco), which is now privately managed. Guysuco exports much of the sugar to the European Union, where, under international agreements, Guyana can get a better price than in other parts of the world.

The fertile soil, sunny climate, and abundance of water on the coast are good conditions for growing rice. More than 15,000 farmers work in the industry. Many are small family-run businesses that rent land from the government. There are two rice seasons—the spring crop and the autumn crop. The rice seedlings are prepared in special beds. Some twenty-five to fifty days later, farmers plant them in fields, or paddies,

Rice is a major crop, both for export and as a staple in the Guyanese diet.

where they remain covered by water during the growing season. The land is drained and dried before harvesting, when workers cut much of the crop by hand with a sickle. In some regions, oxen and water buffalo are still used to take the harvested rice to the mills. In the mills, the rice seed is removed from its husk and laid out to dry in

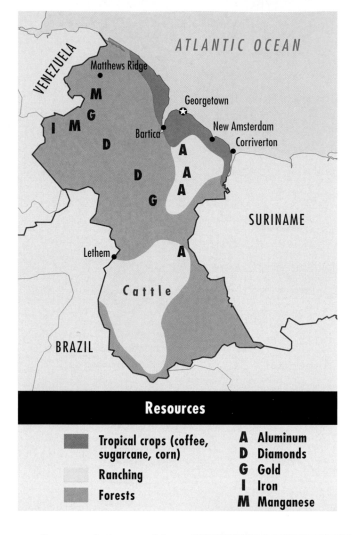

Resources

- ▮ Tropical crops (coffee, sugarcane, corn)
- ▯ Ranching
- ▮ Forests

A	Aluminum
D	Diamonds
G	Gold
I	Iron
M	Manganese

Locally grown fruits are sold within Guyana.

the sun. It is then put into bags for export. In the 1990s modern machinery and some new varieties of rice have helped increase the amount of rice cultivated.

More than 80 percent of the rice is sold overseas, but it is also an everyday part of the Guyanese family diet. The Guyanese also grow other crops for their own use. These include the root vegetable cassava (manioc), coffee, cocoa, cotton, tobacco, corn, and a wide variety of fruit and other vegetables. Herds of dairy cattle are kept mostly on the coast, while farmers raise beef cattle in some areas of the Rupununi. Some rural families and farmers also keep pigs, goats, sheep, and poultry.

Fishing and Forestry

With its many rivers and seacoast, Guyana should have a prosperous fishing industry. However, fish is mostly caught and sold in local markets. The exception has been shrimp. The catch in the 1980s improved so greatly that it became an important export. Investors have now started shrimp farms along the coast, and shrimp boats are a regular sight in Georgetown harbor.

Forests cover about three-quarters of Guyana and are a rich source of timber. There are thought to be more than one thousand species of trees there. The best of these, for commercial use, are the hardwoods such as greenheart, which is not affected by pests or bad climate conditions. It provides excellent timber for making furniture. Other trees are cut for

Shrimp are such an important export that ponds have been started to keep up with demand.

Weights and Measures

Guyana adopted the metric system in 1997, but British imperial measures are still widely used.

Logging operations in the Guyanese interior.

plywood or used as timber in the building trade. The industry, though, has always been small. It is difficult to get workers and equipment into the forest and to get the sawn timber out. However, in the 1990s, the Guyanese government, and private and foreign investors began some large-scale projects. Their aim is to create a profitable timber industry without endangering too much of the native forest.

Rivers and Ferryboats

The Guyanese have always relied on rivers to get them from one place to another. In the interior, canoes and small riverboats carry people and produce. Near the coast, oceangoing vessels and ferries cross the large river estuaries. Today, a good 186-mile (300-km) road runs along much of the coast, but it still has to cross three major rivers. Only the Demerara River has a bridge, the Harbor Bridge (right), which is one of the longest floating bridges in the world. The other two rivers, the Essequibo and the Berbice, have to be crossed by ferry. And the only way of getting from Guyana to Suriname across the Courantyne River is by ferry.

Mining

The mineral bauxite is used for making the metal aluminum. Guyana has huge bauxite deposits. They include the highest grade of the mineral, and at one time Guyana was the world's leading producer of this grade. But the industry went into decline in the 1980s due to a fall in world prices, bad management, and workers' strikes. In 1982 the one processing plant, in Linden, was closed. In 1992 the industry passed back into private hands. Since then more mines have opened, improvements have been made to transport the bauxite from the interior to the coast, and exports have improved.

The mining success story of the 1990s was gold. New government policies encouraged private and foreign investors to explore on a large scale, and Guyana now has the second-largest gold mine in South America. It is the Omai gold mine,

Power lines carry expensive, imported power to Guyana.

located south of Georgetown. In the year 2000 it produced about two-thirds of the country's gold. With modern development and production technology, several companies are helping to make gold the country's most important export. Diamonds are also mined, though many of the gems are illegally smuggled out of the country.

One of the main problems facing Guyana's industries is a lack of energy. No reserves of oil have been found. The numerous rivers would be good for hydroelectricity, but the government has not had

Pork-knockers

For many years men, and sometimes women, have ventured into the interior of Guyana to search for gold, diamonds, and other minerals. They endured terrible conditions, working knee-deep in rivers and mud, hoping to find nuggets or the glimmer of a precious rock. They were known as pork-knockers. It seems the prospectors were given this name because in the old days they survived on rations of rice and salted pork tails. When they ate the pork tails, they would talk of "knocking the pork." Every pork-knocker dreams of discovering a shout, or strike, of gold and diamonds. A few have, like Ocean Shark, an Amerindian miner whose picture is painted on a bank ceiling in Georgetown.

the money to build dams and power plants. Electricity is expensive and only available along the coastal plain. As a result, Guyana has to import most of its energy, which is very costly.

Tourism

Guyana may not be everyone's choice for a holiday, but for anyone with a sense of adventure and a love of animals and plants, it is a great challenge. Tourism in Guyana is a growing industry that brings in much-needed foreign exchange. Offered to tourists are magnificent scenery, including the Kaieteur and other waterfalls; great savannas; the wilderness of the Guyana highlands; rain forests that have not been disturbed; masses of wildlife; and large ranches where tourists can experience cowhand life.

To make tourism work, Guyana needs to build more hotels and better roads. Many parts of the interior can only be reached by plane or boat, which is expensive for most travelers. But the conditions are ideal for eco-tourism, which allows tourists to visit remote or virgin areas while at the same time ensuring the environment is not damaged.

Tourists enjoy one of Guyana's many waterfalls.

Rupununi Weavers

A few years ago some Wapishana Indians in the Rupununi revived an age-old tradition of making cotton hammocks. It takes six hundred hours of weaving to make each hammock from rain forest cotton. They are a beautiful example of tribal art.

The skill would have disappeared had it not been for a young British volunteer worker. He presented one of these hammocks to the Royal Academy in London, and the word spread. Queen Elizabeth II and the Duke of Edinburgh were presented with one during a state visit to Guyana in 1994, and the Smithsonian Institution in Washington, D.C., has one in its South American Textile Art Collection.

Soon a link to the outside commercial world was established. The Guyana Telephone Company provided the weavers with a satellite link, computers, and a Web site. The story of the weavers was soon told by the international press and the *New York Times*. Enough orders were generated that the Wapishana could buy a tractor. The downside has been that the Wapishana leaders see cyberspace as a threat to their authority. But the hammock weavers have pressed on, and the Rupununi Weavers Society is flourishing.

Land of Six Peoples

T RAVELERS IN THE EARLY TWENTIETH CENTURY DESCRIBED British Guiana as the "Land of Six Peoples." Of these, only the Amerindians were native to the land. The others were descended from the British colonists, African slaves, and East Indian, Portuguese, and Chinese immigrants who arrived during the nineteenth century.

Guyana is still a land of six peoples, but there have been changes. Today the majority of people are of East Indian or African descent, and there are only small numbers of Europeans and Chinese. However, marriage between these peoples has produced a group of about 12 percent of the population who are of mixed color. People of mixed African and European descent are *mulattoes*, and children of African and East Indian parents are *douglahs*.

When Christopher Columbus first arrived in the New World in 1492, he thought he had reached the Indies. He mistakenly called the people of the New World "Indians," a term still used in Central and South America today. But in Guyana, the native Americans became known as Amerindians, short for American Indians, so as not to confuse them with the East Indians. Nine tribes of Amerindians have survived in Guyana.

Opposite: **Amerindian children line up to extend a traditional greeting.**

Most Guyanese are of East Indian or African descent.

Who Lives in Guyana?

East Indian	49%
African	32%
Mixed	12%
Amerindian	6%
White and Chinese	1%

Makushi villagers relax outside their hut.

Amerindians

Fewer than 50,000 Amerindians live in Guyana. They represent about 6 percent of the population. The nine Amerindian tribes are the Akawaio, Arawak, Carib, Makushi, Patamona, Arekuna, Waiwai, Wapishana, and Warrau. They are spread widely across Guyana.

The most isolated, the Waiwai, live in the far south near the source of the Essequibo River and the border of Brazil. The Wapishana and the Makushi live in the southern Rupununi Savanna. In the center-west of the country a small group of Patamona live close to the source of the Potaro River.

The other groups all live in the northern part of Guyana. The most numerous are the Arawak, who have several communities not far from the coast, ranging from the Barima River in the west to the Demerara River in the east. Also near the Barima River are the Caribs and a community of Warrau. More Warrau are found in the east on the lower Courantyne River, close to the Suriname border. The Akawaio live in two locations, several hundred miles apart, on the

Berbice and Mazaruni Rivers. West of the Akawaio, on the Mazaruni River and close to the Venezuelan border, is a small group of Arekuna.

In some ways, Amerindians live as they have done for centuries. Some still hunt and fish with bows and arrows, and they use palm thatch and hardwoods to build their homes and canoes. They clear areas of forest to grow crops. Their most important crop is the root vegetable cassava. Cassava contains a poisonous juice which when boiled can be used as a preservative known as casareep. Once this has been extracted, grated cassava is mixed with water and cooked like a large pancake on an open fire. Other crops include bananas, coconuts, peanuts, and papaya.

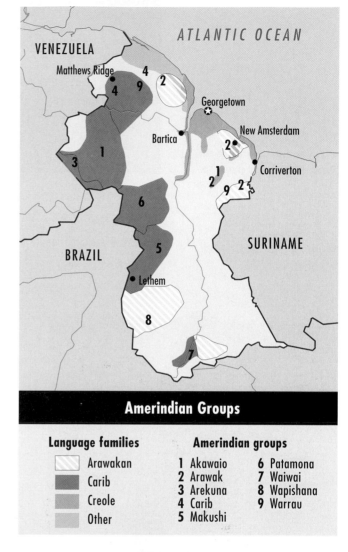

Amerindian Groups

Language families

▨	Arawakan
▧	Carib
▨	Creole
▨	Other

Amerindian groups

1	Akawaio	6	Patamona
2	Arawak	7	Waiwai
3	Arekuna	8	Wapishana
4	Carib	9	Warrau
5	Makushi		

This Amerindian boy fishes using a traditional bow and arrow.

This village provides stability and security to the Amerindians that live in it.

Working on a cattle ranch is not an easy job.

At one time, Amerindians were always on the move in the forests, grasslands, and mountains. Over the centuries, their unique knowledge and skill enabled them to survive on the natural resources of the environment, while at the same time not endangering them. Today most are settled in communities or villages, and some have been relocated to large reservations.

From the time the Europeans arrived, it was inevitable that Amerindian life would change. Early on, missionaries damaged aspects of their culture while trying to convert them to Christianity. The Arawaks, the most outgoing of the groups, and the Caribs worked for the colonists on the sugar plantations and helped them by catching runaway black slaves. In the Kanuku Mountains, the Makushi collected *balata*, the gum of the bullet wood tree, and sold it to traders. More recently, Amerindians have found jobs as loggers in the forests, on cattle ranches, or as laborers mining gold or diamonds. They remain at the lower end of Guyanese society. They are badly paid, often taken advantage of, and their life is primitive and tough.

However, earning money has enabled Amerindians to buy goods in Guyana's markets that have changed their lifestyle. Many now wear western dress—trousers and shirts for the men, simple dresses for the women. More and more dwellings are being constructed with nontraditional materials such as concrete and aluminum sheets. Hand-crafted canoes are being replaced by boats with outboard motors, and guns are used alongside bows and arrows.

Education too has brought change to the Amerindians. If a village does not have a school, Amerindian children will paddle many miles every day along a river to reach one. Most have basic reading and writing skills. Amerindians also have a growing knowledge of modern technology—bicycles, radios, calculators, and even computers are no longer unfamiliar items.

Traditionally, Amerindians have treated illness, cuts, or bruises with berries, leaves, or saps from plants and trees. Today, some villages have medical posts but most are badly equipped. Amerindian communities generally do

Amerindian children attending school

not have electricity or plumbing systems. Doctors seldom visit, so for very serious cases, Amerindians have to make journeys that can last days to get to the nearest hospital. For reasons like this, more and more Amerindians are looking to settle in the towns; however, they find it difficult to get work.

Although some Amerindians have chosen to join the cash economy, others believe it is more important to fight for the right to own their own land. Amerindians may have lived on the land for centuries, but it is difficult to prove they have a legal right to it. So when a new rich mineral deposit is found or a timber company begins logging or a new road is cut through the forest, the Amerindians are forced to move on. Violent protests have taken place. An organization known as the Amerindian People's Association helps Amerindians to fight for their rights as Guyanese citizens and to get positive answers to the land issue.

Afro-Guyanese

Most of the African slaves brought to Guyana in the seventeenth and eighteenth centuries originated from the Guinea

Grand Piano in the Savanna

The Waiwai recently asked a British scientific and exploration society for a grand piano. It seemed an extraordinary request since no Waiwai knew how to play, but the society, which had already provided doctors, dentists, and medical supplies, was determined to fulfill it. A piano was donated, and a medical doctor who could play joined the team. After months of planning, the expedition set off with the piano. They arrived in Georgetown, and from there the piano was flown for two-and-a-half hours into the interior. The piano was then strapped to a sledge to drag it across the savanna, before the final lap on a 30-foot (more than 9 m)-long dugout canoe. It arrived in one piece, much to the joy of everyone concerned.

coast of West Africa. They soon lost their ties and traditions with their homeland. When slavery was abolished in the early nineteenth century, some stayed on the plantations, but others got together, bought land, and set up villages. They realized that only by owning land upon which they could build their own homes and farms would they be free of the planters. By 1850 they were the largest group in the population, and they remained so well into the next century.

Today, in the towns, Afro-Guyanese work at every level of Guyanese society. Some of the most successful are lawyers, teachers, and doctors, while others have important positions in government. But for the majority life is a constant struggle. They may have part-time jobs or no job at all. Unemployment is very high. Those who get work, perhaps in factories, at the docks, or driving taxis, often need to have more than one job to make a living. Trading from stalls in the street is another option, one that women often do.

This woman sells snacks and drinks from a roadside stand.

A mother and daughter dressed in their Sunday best.

Afro-Guyanese women are very independent and combine work and homelife. Their children are always well dressed, especially on Sundays, when families go to church. Young boys wear crisp white shirts with long trousers, and the girls have brightly colored dresses and wear bows in their hair. In general, the Afro-Guyanese have an easygoing, laid-back charm typical of the Caribbean. There is nothing they enjoy more than an evening of music and dance.

Indo-Guyanese

There are now more Indo-Guyanese, or East Indians, than Afro-Guyanese. Since arriving in Guyana over 150 years ago, they have become successful businesspeople and rice farmers. For many years, while the country was still British Guiana,

Languages

The official language of Guyana is English. But the first language of many people, spoken from birth, is Guyanese Creole English, or "Creolese." The language is based on English but has absorbed African, Dutch, Amerindian, and other words. Many Amerindians speak Creolese but they also have their own languages, such as Arawaks, Caribs, and Warau. Altogether thirteen different languages are spoken in Guyana.

Here are a few Creolese phrases:

Ah deh bout.	I'm still around.
Deh pon heights.	He's into something.
Doan feel no way.	Don't take it seriously.
Fires pon you!	Nonsense, I rebuke you!
Humble up.	Take it easy; cool down.
Sus it out.	Examine a matter closely.
To su-su.	To speak in secret, to gossip.

Here are a few Guyanese proverbs:

Hurry, hurry, spile yuh curry.	Look before you leap.
Good gubby nah ah float ah top.	Good things do not come easily.
Every rope got two ends.	Every story has two sides.
If yuh eye nuh see, yuh mouth nuh must talk.	You must see for yourself before you talk.

the East Indian community kept themselves apart from the rest of society. A few were Muslims, but the religion of most was Hindu. At that time, some children received only a limited education because their parents preferred not to send them to Christian schools, and often they were needed to work on the family farm. But others, especially boys, were educated in the Hindi language at their local temples.

The situation changed by the middle of the twentieth century. As soon as the East Indians realized the value of education, they progressed quickly. When their home country, India, became independent in 1947, it gave them new confidence and pride. Although the British still controlled Guyana and opportunities were very limited, especially for East Indians in rural areas, they took more interest in politics and the move toward independence.

Today in Georgetown wealthy Indo-Guyanese business-people own shops, garages, cinemas, and offices. Others, less prosperous, run market stalls alongside those of the Afro-Guyanese and rent shops to run their own small businesses. However, much of the Indo-Guyanese wealth is still in the profitable family-run rice farms that they own along the coast and on the outskirts of the towns. Within the family circle, their first language is Guyanese Creole. They have

An Indo-Guyanese shop owner in front of his store.

kept their Hindu religion and celebrate with traditional Hindu festivals.

Chinese

Between 1853 and 1879 a total of 13,541 laborers arrived in British Guiana from China as indentured laborers. By 1900 the Chinese population was down to only 3,000. This was because so few of the immigrants were women.

When they first arrived, the Chinese had a hard time and were alienated from the rest of the population. But once they were freed, those who chose to stay and settle became successful mainly as shopkeepers and businesspeople. Many of their descendants, with the advantage of a better education, entered the professions as lawyers, teachers, and doctors and worked in government. One of them was Arthur Chung, the first president of Guyana, from 1970 to 1980.

The Chinese languages and most Chinese customs, including religion, disappeared. Chinese people married both East Indians and Africans, and with each successive generation the Chinese have become more and more absorbed into Guyanese society. They are no longer a distinct, separate group.

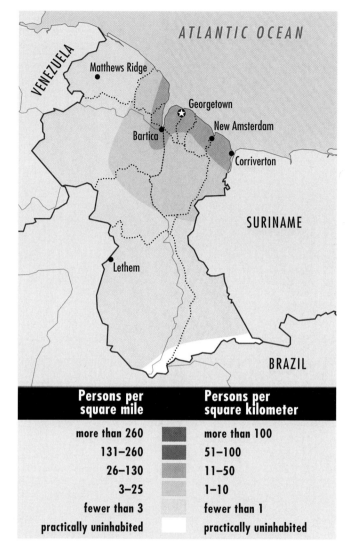

Persons per square mile		Persons per square kilometer
more than 260		more than 100
131–260		51–100
26–130		11–50
3–25		1–10
fewer than 3		fewer than 1
practically uninhabited		practically uninhabited

Population of major cities (1999 est.)

Georgetown	275,000
Linden	35,000
New Amsterdam	25,000

Faiths from East and West

GUYANA, THE LAND OF SIX PEOPLES, IS ALSO THE LAND of as many if not more spiritual ways. For the Amerindians, time is moving them forward relentlessly.

A century ago the people along the Essequibo River believed that evil spirits lived in rocks, and one rock called *paiwari-kaira* was especially bad. This large rock sat on a natural pillar in midstream, and no person dared look at it. To even mention the rock brought misfortune, and it was a taboo subject in the very strictest way. Other rocks, streams, and waterfalls also were regarded with awe.

All the Amerindian people of the Guianas had centuries-old beliefs attached to spirits that came from animals or trees. Frogs, monkeys, tapirs, birds, insects—all kinds of animals—and the fruits of the trees were part of their ancient beliefs.

Opposite: **Uyara, water spirit of Guyana**

Major Religious Festivals and Holidays

Hindu and Muslim festivals follow a lunar calendar. Most religious festivals are also national holidays.

Chinese Spring Festival	January to early Februray
Id al-Adha (festival of sacrifice)	Last month of the Islamic calendar
Phagwah (Hindu)	Usually in March
Easter	March or April
Yum-an-Nabi (Muslim)	May or June
Diwali (Hindu "festival of light")	October or November
Ramadan (Muslim month of fast)	Ninth month of Islamic calendar
Id al-Fitr	End of Ramadan
Christmas	December 25

Life was simple, and although the Amerindians faced many natural dangers, they cared deeply for their forests and the natural world, for otherwise the spirits would be harmed.

Christianity

With the arrival of the Europeans, new ideas were introduced, though tribes in the interior were unaffected for some time. Europeans brought Christianity and its calendar of holy days. About 50 percent of the population today is Anglican, but the few people of Portuguese descent are usually Roman Catholic. A small number of Chinese are Christians.

In modern Guyana the Christian community observes the main feasts of Good Friday, Easter, and Christmas. Plans for Christmas begin early with the preparations for feasting. Cakes are mixed and baked, presents are bought or made at home, and several types of traditional drinks are prepared. Ginger beer is a favorite and so is a wine-colored drink for children made from the sorrel plant. The main dish for the family gathering is "pepper pot" often served alongside the Portuguese speciality of garlic pork.

Christmas decorations brighten up Georgetown.

Guyanese Christians and others decorate their homes with trees and send Christmas cards. Parties, dances, and family reunions continue for several days. Boxing Day, December 26, which has no direct religious connection, is a day of rest and a national holiday.

Easter, the greatest and oldest feast of the Christian church, is celebrated with a religious day on Easter Sunday followed by a national holiday on Easter Monday. On this holiday, the children of Georgetown have fun when they gather by the seawall to fly kites, a colorful sport that over the years has become a tradition.

Hinduism

When the indentured laborers began to arrive from the East, they brought their own religious beliefs. These beliefs have survived to the present day. Most of the people of

A Hindu temple in Georgetown

Indian origin are Hindus, followers of Hinduism, the world's oldest faith. Unlike Christianity, Hinduism does not have a single founder. Instead, it evolved over a period of 5,000 years, drawing together religious ideas from many parts of India. Guyanese Hindus observe many of the festivals followed in India today. Temples are used for meetings and prayers.

The festival of colors, or *Phagwah*, is the Guyanese version of Holi, the spring festival observed in much of northern India. The festival is very popular with young people.

Colored water is thrown on passersby during Phagwah.

Phagwah is the moment for enjoying life and getting to know more friends. Prayers are said at the beginning, but the fun comes from the lively sport of throwing colored water or colored powders at one another. Young people run around the houses or village streets smearing friends, or sometimes even strangers' faces and bodies with the colors. As they do at other festivals, the Hindus make sweets that they can give to friends. Vegetarian dishes are prepared and shared. No traveler is ever turned away.

Festival of Lights

Diwali, one of the most beautiful Hindu festivals, has become a national holiday in Guyana, celebrated during October or November each year. The festival is also known as Divali or Deepvali. It honors Lakshmi, the Hindu goddess of wealth, and the very important and ancient belief of Lord Rama's return from a fourteen-year exile. Diwali, or "string of lights," is celebrated with many different kinds of light, and specially made sweets, some scented with fragrant seeds, are handed out. In their homes, Hindu families offer prayers and burn *diyas*, small earthenware lamps with candles or oil. Shops and public buildings are decorated with lights. Fireworks sparkle at night, and fairs are held in Georgetown and Berbice.

Islam

Not all the Indian people are Hindus; about 15 percent are Muslims, who follow the Islamic faith. This religion has its origins in the Middle East with the followers of the prophet Muhammad. Islam reached India in the tenth century with Arab traders and the Muslim conquest of the region.

Indo-Guyanese Muslims are Sunni, one of the two main branches of the Islamic faith, and they follow the principal Muslim beliefs and festivals. They have built mosques for meetings and prayer. Ramadan, the most important month of the year, is observed by more than a billion followers all over the world. It is the historic month when the holy book, the Koran (or Qur'an), was revealed to the prophet Muhammad. Ramadan is a time for many prayers and fasting, without even a drink being permitted between sunrise and sunset.

The date of this festival is not fixed by the Gregorian calendar, unlike Christian holidays. Instead, it coincides with the Muslim year, which is based on the phases of the moon. When the new moon is seen at the end of Ramadan, then it is time for the festival of Id al-Adha, the festival of sacrifice.

Another Muslim festival, Yum an-Nabi, is so important that it has been named a national holiday. This is the day commemorating the birthday of Muhammad.

Muslim children study Arabic and the Koran at the Queenstown mosque.

A Mixing of Faiths

One of the interesting things about Guyanese religious practices is the extent to which the faiths coexist. Many Hindus and Muslims, for example, celebrate Christian holy days such as Easter. Hindus in the countryside also attend Christian churches on important Christian occasions, even though they have not converted to Christianity but maintain their own faith. This coexistence is evident in others ways too. For example, if a Muslim family is having a wedding, they will ask a Hindu neighbor to help with the cooking and feeding of their Hindu guests. This is because Muslims eat beef and Hindus do not. So Hindu guests will be guaranteed that their dietary preferences are respected.

Out of Africa

Slaves from Africa were taught the ways of Jesus by the plantation owners, and today many are devout Christians. Very little of the original African culture has survived. A few men and women, though, still practice the witchcraft of *obeah*, a system of beliefs, and are believed to have the power to communicate with spirits. The obeah believers use their powers to cure people or to frighten people with magic. Although modern Guyana permits complete religious freedom, some of the practices of African witchcraft are outlawed.

Spreading the Word

For centuries the words of Jesus were carried to the people by missionaries who traveled by canoe or trekked through the forests. Some still work in the same way, though more and more

Jonestown

The most notorious moment in the recent history of religious freedom in Guyana occurred in 1978: the Jonestown Massacre.

A cult from the United States known as the People's Temple of Christ built a settlement in the far north of the country near Matthews Ridge, beyond the Cuyuni River. U.S. followers of an Indianapolis preacher named James Warren Jones (photo), cleared the forest and built homes and a church.

The place was named Jonestown after its founder. More than 1,000 cult members moved to Jonestown believing they would lead a communal, simple way of life far from the pressures of the modern world. In 1978 reports reached the United States that some of the people were being held against their will. When a U.S. congressman from California, Leo Ryan, went to investigate with three journalists, Jones ordered them killed and soon after encouraged 913 members of the cult to take their own lives. The mass suicide on November 18, 1978, including Jones' own, has become known as the Jonestown Massacre.

the airplane has taken over. Missionaries with no more than a Bible are rare today; their place has been taken by teachers, nurses, and doctors who carry their faith and healing to distant areas such as the Waiwai communities in the Acarai Mountains.

One U.S. missionary group specializes in translating the Amerindian languages and producing works from the gospels that are easily understood by the tribes. Such work is painstakingly slow, and the translators may spend years with a tribe, returning to the United States just once every three or four years. With the spread of radio, then television, and now the Internet, many evangelical churches have reached more people. Some have a strong following, especially among the Afro-Guyanese.

Arts and Sporting Traditions

THE SCHOLAR DR. DENIS WILLIAMS (1923–1998), LIKE several of his Guyanese contemporaries, excelled in more than one of the arts. He was a multitalented painter, novelist, museum curator, and anthropologist. As a young man, he won an art scholarship to study in London, and then taught there. From 1957 to 1967 he was in Africa teaching art and art history. It was in the Sudan in 1968 that his interest in archaeology was first aroused.

He returned to Guyana in the 1970s determined to learn, as he put it, "about the who and how, as well as the when of the arts of the Guyana Indians." He studied ancient petroglyphs, the drawings on rocks done by ancient tribes, and

Opposite: **Wood-carved figure of men with a palm tree**

Guyanese scholar and artist Denis Williams

Handwoven straw goods
reflect ancient skills.

he excavated pots and artifacts that helped explain their way of life. Later he was able to use his experience and knowledge to help create the Walter Roth Museum, so that the next generation could learn about their ancestors.

Some aspects of the culture and crafts of the early people have survived to this day. Amerindians still weave baskets and hammocks and are skilled in making clay pots, which they decorate with complex designs. The name of one of Guyana's best-known festivals, *Mashramani*, or Mash, derives from an Amerindian word meaning "the celebration of a job well done." It now takes place on February 23, Republic Day, and features bands, dance routines originating from Africa, and masquerade characters like Mad Bull and Mother Sally.

The Walter Roth Museum

Named after a British doctor and geologist who was posted in Guyana in 1909, the Walter Roth Museum is on Main Street in Georgetown. It was founded in 1974 with the collections of Denis Williams. Other collections were added later.

Moving through the rooms, visitors can see many different artifacts well displayed with valuable information about the original tribes who created them. Paintings of the tribespeople in traditional dress also give some idea of what the ancient people looked like. Some, like the Waiwai men, have spectacular feathered headdresses. Alongside the paintings are Waiwai combs made of pine needles and monkey bone. There are also old Makushi sandals, made from the *ite* or *moriche* palm.

Pottery bowls and burial urns of the Akawaio, Patamona, Makushi, and Caribs are on display. In the Wapishana section, there are diagrams and drawings of fish traps that date back 4,000 years. Traps like these are still used by the Wapishana. Little is known of the Arekuna except for their knowledge of the blowpipe, a devastating weapon when used skillfully (above). Petroglyphs are explained: for example, a man attached to a deer represents twenty deer. The caption on one describes how the carvings on the rock count the number of animals taken from the forest on a day's hunting. The Arawak had their own type of rock engraving, called *timehri*. They were the most advanced of the tribes, and there are descriptions of the way they farmed in the coastal swamps.

The museum also has a library, publishes a journal every year, and runs educational programs, some especially designed to get schoolchildren interested in archaeology.

Artists

Guyanese artists have been greatly influenced by their native land and people. Paintings reflect the culture of the Amerindians and the diversity of peoples who have settled in Guyana. The painter Aubrey Williams (1926–1990) spent time with the Warrau, and they were a great influence on him. Hearing the Amerindians talk about color and form, Williams "started to understand what art really is."

Two other well-known artists are Ronald Savory and Stanley Greaves. Savory's work in particular has brought the unknown interior of the country to the attention of city dwellers. Greaves's art has changed over the years. One of his early works was a series of figurative paintings called *People of the Pavement*, after which he focused on abstract painting. More recently he has produced a series of what he calls "mini-paintings" in which he experiments with the size and scale of objects. Greaves is also a wood-carver and potter.

Another artist, Philip Moore, is a sculptor. He is well known for his wood sculptures, which show African influences, and he is the creator of the 15-foot (4.6-m)-high brass statue in Georgetown of Cuffy, leader of the 1763 slave rebellion. There are permanent displays of the work of artists and sculptors in the National Cultural Center in Georgetown.

Writers

One of Guyana's best-known writers is Edgar Mittelholzer (1909–1965). He wrote the historical series called *Kaywana Family Trilogy*, which traces the history of one Guyanese family over 350 years. He also wrote *My Bones and My Flute*, a ghost story about a Dutch plantation owner whose soul would not rest until he was given a Christian burial. Other writers are Wilson Harris and E. R. Braithwaite (see page 126).

Most Guyanese writers have spent much time outside Guyana, and Walter Rodney was no exception. He studied history in Jamaica and in London. A move to Africa prompted his lifelong mission to find a better life for black people. His first and perhaps best-known book, *How Europe Underdeveloped Africa*, shows how Britain and other colonial powers affected Africa with poverty and slavery of the black people. Rodney eventually returned to Guyana in 1974 and entered politics. But his opposition to the ruling

Writer Theodore Wilson Harris

Wilson Harris, as this writer is usually known, was born in 1921 in New Amsterdam, British Guiana. His background was unusual. He was descended from Afro-Caribbeans, Arawak Indians, and Europeans. He was educated at Queen's College in Georgetown. While Harris was still a young man, his father vanished in the Guyana rain forest. Perhaps influenced by this, he chose a career as a government surveyor and spent much of his time between 1942 and 1958 in Guyana's remote but beautiful savannas and rain forests.

During the 1950s he published some poems, and in 1959 he moved to London. There he began to write fiction, often using his experiences in Guyana's interior as a background to his stories. In the early 1960s he wrote and published *The Guyana Quartet*. This consisted of four volumes of which the first, *The Palace of the Peacock*, takes up the challenge of nature. Many people still regard this as his masterpiece. Harris's novels have a very mystical and magical style to them. Fantasy, dreams, and reality are all intertwined.

Between 1977 and 1990 he wrote other novels, six of which were published as triologies—sets of three volumes. These are perhaps his best-known works. The first triology is based in London and includes *Da Silva's da silva's Cultivated Wilderness*, *The Tree of the Sun*, and *The Angel at the Gate*. The second trilogy is composed of *Carnival*, *The Infinite Rehearsal*, and *The Four Banks of the River of Space*. Harris also wrote many short stories and essays.

government cost him his life; he was assassinated in 1980. Before his death he had completed the first volume of what would have been the work of his life, *History of the Guyanese Working People.*

A number of younger writers draw upon their own early lives growing up in British Guiana. Their work includes the humorous account of comic and unusual characters in Bernard L. Heydorn's *Walk Good Guyana Boy*, and Noel Compton Bacchus's *Guyana Farewell*, which is full of nostalgic memories, like the yearly school summer holiday. The family would leave at the crack of dawn on a small steam-driven wooden train, on a hazardous journey to stay with relatives up country.

Among the country's outstanding poets are Martin Carter, who wrote *Poems of Resistance*, and A. J. Seymour, who wrote *I Was Born in Georgetown.*

A Musical Mix

Guyanese music is a mix influenced by African, Caribbean, Amerindian, European, North American, and East Indian music. Amerindians use bamboo flutes and drums made from rawhide for their own native ceremonies. Indo-Guyanese communities have traditional ankle and hand bells for their dances, while downtown Georgetown nightclubs thump out North American and European pop music.

Perhaps the most widespread popular music is the Caribbean-style calypso. It is a special kind of song, written in dialect. The words are witty and often make fun of politics and people. Calypso competitions are held during Mashramani.

Calypso is usually backed by traditional steel drum bands, though during Mashramani fife or traditional flute bands take part. Another kind of music very popular in Guyana is chutney. Chutney songs are composed partly in English and partly in Hindi. They derive from traditional Indian folk songs, but have touches of calypso. They can be rather sassy and are performed at special events and parties.

Georgetown steel drum band

Queh Queh Shower

Queh Queh is a celebration that usually takes place a week or two before a wedding. It is a Guyanese custom that has its origins in Africa. Men and women take part in a ceremony that includes African dancing and drumming, and lots of good food. The music includes traditional songs that often have naughty lyrics. They are sung by the older members of the family as a sort of encouragement to the couple who are getting married.

Sports in Guyana

The Guyanese are passionate about cricket. It is a game, not unlike baseball, with batsmen, bowlers, and fieldsmen. Two teams compete against each other to see who can score the most runs. A bowler pitches the ball at a batsman, trying to hit the stumps or wicket behind him. If the batsman hits the ball well enough, he runs the length of the pitch and scores a run. Fieldsmen try to run out the batsman by hitting the wicket with the ball before the batsman reaches it.

The game was introduced by the British and has been played on the Georgetown Cricket Club grounds, commonly

A match at the Georgetown Cricket Club

This schoolgirl is playing in a cricket match.

known as Bourda, since 1883. Bourda is the world's only international cricket grounds that is below sea level, and many important matches have been played there. The large crowd of spectators takes part in the traditional clapping whenever a batsman is caught or bowled out.

Cricket is played in every part of Guyana, though Berbice is known to produce many of the best players. Boys and girls start at a very early age, using sticks or pieces of wood for bats. They play on any spare patch of ground. Clive Lloyd is Guyana's most famous cricketer, but today's successful young players include Carl Hooper, Shivnarine Chanderpaul, and Reon King.

Rugby was also introduced to Guyana by the British, and other team sports include soccer, volleyball, netball, hockey, and tennis. Spectator sports include bicycle racing, horse racing, and car racing, with Guyana's Dakota track on the international car-racing circuit. There is also plenty of opportunity for swimming, sailing, water-skiing, and white-water rafting. Guyana's national indoor game is dominoes.

Cricketer Clive Lloyd

Clive Lloyd is six foot, five inches tall, has a large mustache, and wears thick glasses. His eyes were damaged when, at age twelve, he tried to break up a school fight. He may not look like a world-class cricketer, but he is the most successful captain ever to lead the West Indies team in test matches. Test matches are played between a number of countries, including England, India, Australia, and the West Indies.

Lloyd was born in Georgetown in 1944. He made his first-class debut as a left-handed batsman in British Guiana in 1963–1964, and went on to play for the English county Lancashire in 1967. He won his first cap, awarded to players when they first play for their country, for the West Indies in the following year, and in 1974 he was appointed captain. He led his team in a record seventy-four test matches. Of these, the West Indies won thirty-six, lost twelve, and twenty-six were tied.

His personal achievements included scoring many centuries (one hundred runs) in major matches. In

1976 he scored 201 runs in just 120 minutes, still one of the fastest times on record for a double century. He was the first West Indian player to win 100 caps in test cricket. Lloyd was also an accomplished right-arm bowler, taking 114 first-class wickets. He retired as captain in 1985 and since then has worked as a coach, manager, and commentator in Guyana and the West Indies.

Boxing is also very popular. Andrew "Six Heads" Lewis defeated American James Page for the World Boxing Association welterweight championship on February 17, 2001, and became the first Guyanese fighter to win a world title.

Rodeos take place every year on ranches in the savannas. The ranches compete against one another in contests such as milking wild cows, riding bulls, throwing lassos, and tug-of-war. One of the best displays of traditional skills by the Amerindian cowboys is the Rupununi Rodeo. It takes place at Easter time in the town of Lethem and features bronco riding.

Rodeo bull riding

Living and Learning

GUYANA HAS A SMALL POPULATION OF ABOUT 700,000 people. Ninety percent of Guyanese live in the habitable two-thirds of the land along the coast, with about 40 percent of the population in Georgetown, the capital. The only other town of any size on the coast is New Amsterdam, where about 25,000 people live.

The standard of living in Guyana is one of the lowest in South America. Almost a third of the population survive

Opposite: **Most Guyanese are poverty-stricken.**

Luxury homes are few and far between.

below the poverty level. This means that they cannot afford even bare essentials such as food and clothing. A family's home generally reflects its income. In downtown Georgetown there are some fine, large wooden houses, nicely painted, with red-tiled roofs and surrounded by well-kept lawns.

However, for most Guyanese, home is a one- or two-story wooden house, or a wooden house built on concrete posts or poles to raise it above the swamps and annual floods. A modern roof may be made of galvanized tin, but more often roofs are made of some kind of thatch. There is little furniture—a table and some chairs, perhaps, and a hammock or two. Parts of Georgetown, the crowded plantation villages, and rural areas often have no electricity or sanitation. Poverty, especially in Georgetown, has led to increased crime. Muggings and theft are common, and visitors, especially, have to be on their guard.

Education

Guyana has a very high rate of literacy, with more than 98 percent of the people able to read and write. A good system of education existed in British Guiana, but it was mainly children of the middle and upper classes who went beyond primary level. After independence the government set out to change this and opened more secondary schools, especially in rural areas.

In 1976 the government took responsibility for all education, including church and private primary schools. It expected

National Holidays of Guyana

New Year's Day	January 1
Republic Day/Mashramani	February 23
Easter Monday	March or April
Labor Day	May 1
Independence Day	May 26
Caricom Day	First Monday in July
Freedom Day	First Monday in August
Boxing Day	December 26

We Strive for Excellence

Children attend schools lacking supplies and in need of repair.

teachers to support the government's socialist views, and many were not prepared to do that. Hundreds of teachers left the country. Schools have since fallen into disrepair, and there are not enough books and equipment because of lack of funds.

The school year runs from September to July and is divided into Christmas Term, Easter Term, and Summer Term. Children age six to fifteen are required to attend school. They start primary school at age six and attend classes for five hours each day. Primary schools have six grades. Although education is basically free, many children do not go beyond primary school, which finishes when they are about eleven years old. Those who do go further can choose between academic schools and

Games Children Play

Burn out Kids run around the block or field until everyone stops running (burns out); the last one to burn out is the winner.

Catcha A game of tag.

Chinee skipping A game that uses rubber bands joined together; played mostly by girls.

Drop it Peter Boy/Jane and Louisa Both are ring games.

Jummin Another name for marbles.

Littee Similar to jacks, but played with small stones or seeds.

Rounders A game similar to softball, but players run in a circle, not around a diamond.

schools that combine academic and technical studies. They can also choose to go to community high schools that combine academic and vocational subjects, such as agriculture, arts and crafts, or home economics. Guyana's highest educational institution is the University of Guyana, which was founded in 1963.

Kite Flying

Easter Monday is a special time for children—and even some adults—to have fun flying kites. A favorite place to gather is along Georgetown's seawall, and even the prime minister has been known to join in. The kites come in all shapes, sizes, and colors. Many of the kites make a distinctive buzzing sound, which can be very high pitched or simply a low "burr." The sound comes from a piece of string stretched across the top of the kite. The wind catches paper fixed near the string and makes it vibrate. At one time this was just simple fun on a day by the sea, but kite flying has grown into a colorful competition for young and old.

Children under the age of twelve compete in a national test, the Common Entrance Exams, to try to gain a place in one of the more well known secondary schools in the country. The exams are taken very seriously, and students take extra lessons after class, usually paying for a tutor. The test results are announced in the national newspapers. Successful results bestow a great deal of honor on the winners and their schools.

Health

After Guyana became independent, health care declined. The government did not have the funds to maintain hospitals and pay medical staff, and many doctors and nurses left the country. Some diseases that were once under control have returned. These include beriberi and malaria. They are difficult to control. Crowded housing on the plantations and the easily flooded ditches and ponds along the coast provide ideal environments for the malaria-carrying mosquito and the spread of disease. Malaria and other diseases are also in the interior. AIDS is a growing problem, especially among communities along the coast. A government-run program gives some financial help to people who are sick or disabled.

Villagers and farmers grow a wide variety of fruit and vegetables, but many other families cannot grow or afford to buy fresh produce. Nor do they have the money to buy meat or fish, which are necessary for a balanced diet. Without an adequate diet, people become ill, and about a third of Guyanese children under age five are affected by malnutrition.

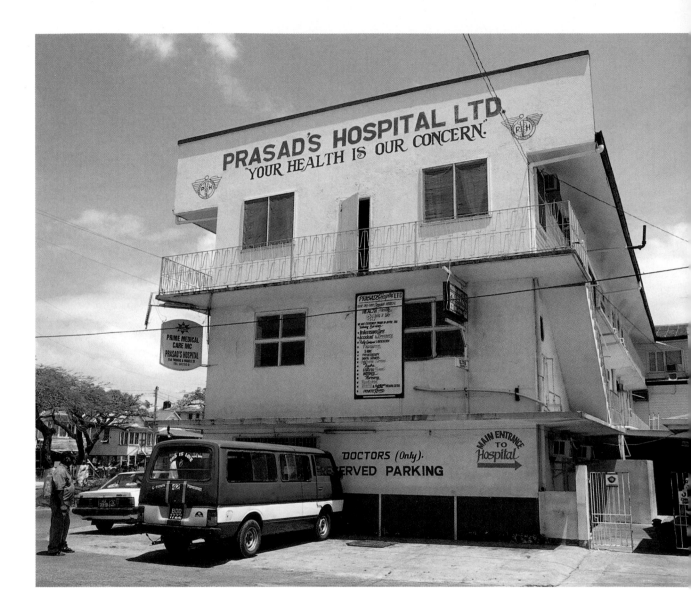

Access to clean running water is equally important to help avoid disease. There are still many households, especially in rural areas, that do not have clean water because local rivers are polluted.

A private hospital in Georgetown

A fruit stand displays a wide assortment of fresh produce.

Local Food

There are few countries that have such a variety of food dishes—not just served in restaurants, but eaten by families at home. The peoples who settled in Guyana still favor dishes that are similar to those of their original countries. Fortunately, the wide range of fruit and vegetables that Guyana produces makes this possible. Alongside the easily recognizable pineapples, mangoes, oranges, grapefruit, and other citrus fruits on market stalls, there are less well known tropical fruits and vegetables. These include sapodillas, with a soft creamy pulp; passionflower fruits such as granadillas; papayas; custard apples; and guavas. Other fruits are jackfruits, with a white pulp often used in spicy dishes; the annonas; and the larger graviola, with numerous glossy seeds enveloped in a sweet pulp.

Typical Guyanese food ranges from hot and spicy curries to Chinese stir-fry, and from African-style dishes that include ingredients such as coconut and root vegetables to Portuguese garlic pork, which is a favorite at Christmastime. Amerindian food is based on cassava. Some people still enjoy the most traditional British dish of roast beef and vegetables.

An Amerindian woman prepares cassava.

A typical African dish is *metemgee* (or *metagee*), which is a mixture of meat and fish with coconut milk, cassava, yams (or local vegetables called *eddoes* or *dasheen*—taro), okra, onion, and plantains. Dumplings are optional. This might be followed by sugar cake, a sweet mixture of coconut, brown sugar, orange peel, and ginger made into little cakes. Another very popular dish is cook-up rice. It is made with cooked and

Metemgee, a traditional Guyanese dish.

Pepper Pot

The nearest thing Guyana has to a national dish is the typical Amerindian pepper pot. It is traditionally eaten at Christmastime. Once it has been cooked, it is kept simmering in the pot so that more ingredients can be added at any time.

Ingredients

2 pounds of stew meat (pork or beef) or brisket	3 heads of clove
2 pig's feet	2 stalks of basil
2 pounds of oxtail	1 stalk of thyme
1 cup *casareep* (see below)	3 garlic cloves
2 red hot peppers, diced	2 ounces of sugar
1 stick cinnamon	1 large onion, chopped
	salt (to taste)

Preparation

Clean the pig's feet thoroughly and put them in a saucepan with water. Cover and bring to a boil. Skim. Simmer for about one hour or until tender. Add the other meat and hot water to cover it. Add all the other ingredients, and simmer until meat is tender. Add salt and sugar.

Casareep juice can be bought in a bottle, or homemade: Peel and grate 1 medium-sized young cassava root. Put into a bowl lined with double-thickness cheesecloth. Bring the end of the cheesecloth together and wring as hard as possible to extract the cassava juice into a bowl. Cook the juice in a heavy skillet on medium-high heat for about one minute, or until the cassareep is smooth and thick enough to hold its shape almost solidly in a spoon.

salt-cured meat, chicken, fish or shrimp, onions, tomatoes, and various herbs. Rice and peas are the basis of many Indian dishes.

Media

The first English-language newspaper, *Royal Essequibo and Demerary Gazette*, appeared regularly every week from August 22, 1796, until 1802, when the colonies were handed back to the Dutch.

Daily newspapers on sale

Today the main newspapers are the *Guyana Chronicle*, the *Stabroek News*, the *Mirror*, and the *New Nation*. The *Stabroek News* is the most independent; the *Chronicle* and the *Mirror* favor the People's Progressive Party; and the *New Nation* is the voice of the People's National Congress.

To Sir with Love

Actor Sidney Poitier starred in *To Sir With Love* (photo), a very successful 1967 film. The story was a best-seller written by Guyanese writer and poet Edward Ricardo Braithwaite. It is based on his experiences teaching underprivileged youngsters in a tough part of London, England. The book was praised for its optimistic view of difficult race relations.

E. R. Braithwaite has also had a successful diplomatic and academic career. As a young man, he fought in World War II as a pilot in the Royal Airforce. He was one of the heroes who flew Spitfire fighters in the Battle of Britain, defending Great Britain from German invasions. He went on to become United Nations ambassador for Guyana when the country first gained independence. Today he is a professor of English at Howard University in Washington, D.C.

Radio is the most widespread form of communication and reaches people in the remotest parts of the country. Guyana has three TV stations. Two are private and can relay U.S. satellite services.

The Future

Guyana is still in many ways the mythical "lost world" and "wild coast" of earlier days. It is one of the least visited and least known countries of South America, yet it contains some very remarkable forests, interesting and varied wildlife, and magnificent scenery. Guyana has a dilemma that is not unusual in developing countries: Everything is in place for a successful eco-tourism industry, but Guyana lacks the funds to develop the necessary roads, hotels, and other facilities to accommodate tourists.

Tourism is perhaps the best, though not the only, bright prospect for the future. Gold production is doing well. There are also valuable mineral resources and timber in the hills and rain forests. The economy is improving, and the government is committed to reducing poverty.

Perhaps the greatest challenge is to bring together the peoples of Guyana. As each generation passes, its varied backgrounds, customs, and cultures become less distinct, and the process of absorbing these differences becomes easier. Rather than being the "land of six peoples," in which social and cultural differences tend to divide people, Guyana is working to become the land of one united people, the Guyanese.

Timeline

Guyanese History		World History	
Inhabited by tribes of Amerindians.	1000 B.C.–A.D. 1000	2500 B.C.	Egyptians build the Pyramids and the Sphinx in Giza.
		563 B.C.	The Buddha is born in India.
		A.D. 313	The Roman emperor Constantine recognizes Christianity.
		610	The Prophet Muhammad begins preaching a new religion called Islam.
		1054	The Eastern (Orthodox) and Western (Roman) Churches break apart.
		1066	William the Conqueror defeats the English in the Battle of Hastings.
		1095	Pope Urban II proclaims the First Crusade.
		1215	King John seals the Magna Carta.
		1300s	The Renaissance begins in Italy.
		1347	The Black Death sweeps through Europe.
		1453	Ottoman Turks capture Constantinople, conquering the Byzantine Empire.
		1492	Columbus arrives in North America.
Columbus possibly sights Guiana coast on his third voyage.	A.D. 1498		
Alonso de Ojeda is the first European to land on South American coast.	1499		
Sir Walter Raleigh searches for El Dorado.	1595	1500s	The Reformation leads to the birth of Protestantism.
Dutch create first settlement.	1616		
Dutch form the West India Company.	1621		
English colonists arrive, led by Lord Willoughby.	1650		
Berbice slave rebellion is led by Cuffy.	1763		
British gain control of Dutch settlements.	1781	1776	The Declaration of Independence is signed.
George Town is named after King George III.	1812	1789	The French Revolution begins.
Colony of British Guiana is created.	1831		
Immigrants from Europe, India, and China arrive.	1834–1917		

Guyanese History

Mount Roraima discovered; slaves freed under the Emancipation Act.	1838
George Town becomes Georgetown.	1841
Kaieteur Falls discovered.	1870
Dispute between Venezuela and British Guiana over lands west of the Essequibo River is resolved in British Guiana's favor.	1899
British Guiana becomes a crown colony.	1928
First political party, the People's Progressive Party founded by Dr. Cheddi Jagan and Forbes Burnham	1953
Forbes Burnham forms his own political party, the People's National Congress.	1955
Guiana becomes an independent nation known as Guyana; Forbes Burnham is the first prime minister.	1966
Guyana becomes a republic.	1970
Guyana adopts socialist policies; Burnham is voted back to power, though accused of rigging the elections.	1970–1980
Jonestown massacre.	1978
Forbes Burnham becomes president, a position he holds until his death in 1985.	1980
Desmond Hoyte becomes president.	1985
Elections won by Cheddi Jagan and People's Progressive Party.	1992
Cheddi Jagan dies and is succeeded by his wife, Janet.	1997
Janet Jagan resigns due to ill health and is succeeded by Bharrat Jagdeo of the PPP.	1999
Bharrat Jagdeo is elected president and Samuel Hinds, prime minister.	2001

World History

1865	The American Civil War ends.
1914	World War I breaks out.
1917	The Bolshevik Revolution brings communism to Russia.
1929	Worldwide economic depression begins.
1939	World War II begins, following the German invasion of Poland.
1945	World War II ends.
1957	The Vietnam War starts.
1969	Humans land on the moon.
1975	The Vietnam War ends.
1979	Soviet Union invades Afghanistan.
1983	Drought and famine in Africa.
1989	The Berlin Wall is torn down, as communism crumbles in Eastern Europe.
1991	Soviet Union breaks into separate states.
1992	Bill Clinton is elected U.S. president.
2000	George W. Bush is elected U.S. president.

Fast Facts

Official name: Cooperative Republic of Guyana

Capital: Georgetown

Official language: English

Georgetown

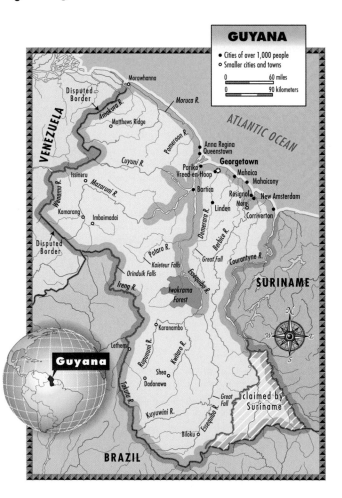

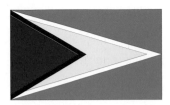

Guyana's flag

Waterfalls of the
Pakaraima Mountains

Major religions: Christianity, Hinduism, Islam

Founding date: 1966

National anthem: "Dear Land of Guyana"

Government: Republic within the British Commonwealth

Chief of state: President

Head of government: Prime minister

Area and dimensions: 83,000 square miles (214,953 sq km); 495 miles (797 km) north to south; 290 miles (467 km) east to west

Geographic coordinates: 5° N, 59° W

Borders: Ocean to the north; Venezuela to the west; Suriname to the east; Brazil to the south and southwest

Highest elevation: Roraima, 9,219 feet (2,835 m)

Lowest elevation: Sea level

Average temperature: 79°F (26°C) in January in Georgetown
81°F (27°C) in July in Georgetown

Average rainfall: 90 inches (229 cm) along the coast; 70 inches (178 cm) far inland

National population (2000 est.): 697,286

Population of largest cities (1999 est.):

Georgetown	275,000
Linden	35,000
New Amsterdam	25,000

Sea turtle

Currency

Famous landmarks:
- ▶ *Kaieteur Falls*, River Potaro
- ▶ *Mount Roraima*, Pakaraima Mountains
- ▶ *Rupununi Savanna*, grasslands in the southwest
- ▶ *Orinduik Falls*, on border with Brazil
- ▶ *Shell Beach*, in the northwest, a protected area for marine turtles and birds
- ▶ *Iwokrama Rain Forest Preserve*, central Guyana

Industry: Gold, bauxite, sugar, and rice are the most important products and represent over 80 percent of exports. Gold is the fastest-growing sector of the economy with the development of the Omai gold mine during the 1990s. Omai is the second largest gold mine in South America. Guyana has huge deposits of bauxite, which is used for making aluminium. Until the discovery of bauxite early in the twentieth century, Guyana's economy was traditionally based on agriculture, particularly sugar. It is still the country's largest industry, employing many thousands of people. Rice was first grown in the late nineteenth century, and the industry was developed along the coast by Chinese families. Tourism is at present a small industry, but there is much potential in Guyana for eco-tourism and adventure holidays.

Currency: Guyanese dollar. There are notes for 20, 100, 500, and 1,000 dollars and coins are for 1, 5, and 10 dollars. In November 2001, U.S.$1 = 180.50 Guyanese dollars.

Weights and measures: Metric system, though British imperial measures are still widely used.

Amerindian children

Cheddi Bharrat Jagan

Literacy:	98 percent

Common words and phrases:	*Ah deh bout.*	I'm still around.
	Sus it out.	Examine a matter closely.
	Humble up.	Take it easy, cool down.

Famous Guyanese:	Edward Ricardo Braithwaite *Scholar, diplomat, and novelist*	(1920–)
	Linden Forbes Sampson Burnham *Politician and Guyana's first president*	(1923–1985)
	Theodore Wilson Harris *Poet and novelist*	(1921–)
	Dr. Cheddi Bharrat Jagan *Politician and president*	(1918–1997)
	Clive Lloyd *Cricketer*	(1944–)
	Edgar Mittelholzer *Writer*	(1909–1965)
	Aubrey Williams *Painter*	(1926–1990)
	Denis Williams *Scholar, painter, novelist, curator, and anthropologist*	(1923–1998)

To Find Out More

Nonfiction

▶ Daly, Vere T. *The Making of Guyana*. London and Oxford: Macmillan Education, 1974.

▶ Daly, Vere T. *A Short History of the Guyanese People*. London and Oxford: Macmillan Education, 1975.

▶ Jermyn, Leslie. *Cultures of the World: Guyana*. Times Media, Singapore, 2000.

Web Sites

▶ **History of Guyana**
www.guyanaguide.com/history.htm
Information on Guyana's history.

▶ **Guyana Scrapbook**
http://geocities.com/TheTropics/
shores/9253/index.html
Entertaining items.

▶ **National Report**
www.sdnp.org.gy/undp-docs/nripd
United Nations development report on Amerindians.

▶ **CIA World Factbook**
www.cia.gov/cia/publications/
factbook/geos/gy.html
Facts and figures on Guyana.

▶ **International Supplements**
www.internationalspecialreports.com
/archives/00/guyana/13.html
Washington Times *report on
Guyana culture.*

▶ **Background Notes: Guyana**
www.state.gov/www/background_
notes/guyana_0800_bgn.html
*U.S. Department of State background
information.*

Organizations and Embassies

▶ **Embassy of Guyana**
3170 Georgetown Place
Washington, DC 20521-3170

▶ **Department of Tourism**
Consulate General of Guyana
866 UN Plaza, 3rd floor
New York, NY 10017
(212) 527-3215

Index

Page numbers in *italics* indicate illustrations.

Meet the Author

MARION MORRISON graduated from the University of Wales and soon after left for Bolivia to work among the Aymara people around Lake Titicaca and the Quechua in other parts of the Andes. In Bolivia she met her husband-to-be, Tony, who was making a series of films about South America for the BBC. Together they have spent the last thirty-eight years traveling in Central and South America, making television films, writing books, and creating a photographic library specializing in the region. They have two children, now grown up, who traveled with them many times in the jungles, mountains, and deserts.

"For this book, I got off to a good start when my husband made a journey to the interior of Guyana," Morrison said. "Life in the backwoods was fascinating not just because of the history but because there was so much that was totally different from the places where I began. Our interest in the Guianas was broadened with journeys to see the 'Lost World.' We filled our bookshelves with volumes about legends, the wildlife, and real people. I find it essential to mix the reading with the travel experience.

"Throughout our travels Tony has been meticulous in keeping detailed notebooks, and it is to these I turn first when beginning a book. Then out comes our map box for a country, town, or historical site. With the main map on the wall in front of me, I can visualize places where we have stopped, perhaps overnight or with a family, or sometimes for just a moment to take a picture.

"That is where our photo library is most useful. I can go to my files and remind myself of the details. Naturally we have not been everywhere, for it would take several lifetimes! So we keep in touch with people who specialize in particular fields. For this I find e-mail has become second nature. It is so fast and now connects us with some of the most remote places. Even people living in far-flung corners can get to an e-mail source.

"For the information about the day-to-day affairs of a country we rely on their government representation in London and belong to societies closely connected with South America. Finally, I make contact with friends and acquaintances who have lived in the country I am writing about. Not only is their knowledge invaluable, but it reminds me of things I have forgotten or overlooked."

When not traveling, Marion Morrison lives in Suffolk, England, with her husband.

Photo Credits